PROCLAMATION:
Aids for Interpreting the
Lessons of the Church Year

LENT

SERIES C

Herman G. Stuempfle, Jr.
and
Peter J. Kearney

FORTRESS PRESS   Philadelphia, Pennsylvania

Library of Congress Catalog Card Number 73–79350

ISBN 0–8006–4053–5

3792H73   Printed in U.S.A.   1–4053

General Preface

Proclamation: Aids for Interpreting the Lessons of the Church Year is a series of twenty-five books designed to help clergymen carry out their preaching ministry. It offers exegetical interpretations of the lessons for each Sunday and many of the festivals of the church year, plus homiletical ideas and insights.

The basic thrust of the series is ecumenical. In recent years the Episcopal church, the Roman Catholic church, the United Church of Christ, and the Lutheran and Presbyterian churches have adopted lectionaries that are based on a common three-year system of lessons for the Sundays and festivals of the church year. *Proclamation* grows out of this development, and authors have been chosen from all of these traditions. Some of the contributors are parish pastors; others are teachers, both of biblical interpretation and of homiletics. Ecumenical interchange has been encouraged by putting two persons from different traditions to work on a single volume, one with the primary responsibility for exegesis and the other for homiletical interpretation.

Despite the high percentage of agreement between the traditions, both in the festivals that are celebrated and the lessons that are appointed to be read on a given day, there are still areas of divergence. Frequently the authors of individual volumes have tried to take into account the various textual traditions, but in some cases this has proved to be impossible; in such cases we have felt constrained to limit the material to the Lutheran readings.

The preacher who is looking for "canned sermons" in these books will be disappointed. These books are one step removed from the pulpit: they explain what the lessons are saying and suggest ways of relating this biblical message to the contemporary situation. As such they are springboards for creative thought as well as for faithful proclamation of the word.

This volume of *Proclamation* has been prepared by Herman G. Stuempfle, Jr., Professor of Homiletics at the Lutheran Theological

Seminary, Gettysburg, Pa., and Fr. Peter J. Kearney, Professor of Old Testament at the Catholic University of America, Washington, D.C. Prof. Stuempfle was editor and homiletician and Fr. Kearney was exegete.

Table of Contents

Ash Wednesday

Lutheran	Roman Catholic	Episcopal	Presbyterian and UCC
Joel 2:12–19	Joel 2:12–18	Joel 2:12–19	Zech. 7:4–10
2 Cor. 5:20*b*–6:2	2 Cor. 5:20–6:2	2 Cor. 5:20*b*–6:10	1 Cor. 9:19–27
Matt. 6:1–6, 16–18 (6:19–21)	Matt. 6:1–6, 16–18	Matt. 6:1–6, 16–21	Luke 5:29–35

EXEGESIS

First Lesson: Joel 2:12–19. The Babylonian exile is past, but now the land has been devastated once more, this time by a locust plague. Joel regards it as an opportunity for conversion to the Lord. This appeal is surely the focus of his message, for only here in his entire book does he employ the typical prophetic expression "says the Lord" (2:12). In his attempt to awaken the people to the urgency of God's message, he used the formula "Yet even now," so typical of Deuteronomic style (e.g., Deut. 4:1); in fact, his message can be understood as largely a development of themes from Deuteronomy, as if reversing the earlier process by which Deuteronomy drew nourishment from the preexilic prophets. Perhaps Joel spoke during the latter part of the fifth century B.C., under the influence of the religious reforms of Nehemiah, which were themselves inspired by Deuteronomy. Joel's appeal for worship from the heart and sincere conversion recalls Deut. 6:5 and 30:2, 10.

He calls the community as a whole to worship, but his appeal is to the piety of each individual. His words recall the weeping and tearing of garments which prompted God to show mercy both to Ahab and Josiah, despite the harsh message of a prophet (1 Kings 21:27–29 and 2 Kings 22:18–20; both passages are probably postexilic additions to the text). Thus he combines a concern for the individual's response together with a profound love of community worship.

His description of God's mercy (2:13) has a cultic origin (cf. Exod. 34:6–8, where Moses worships upon receiving a similar revelation); he regards the grain, wine, and oil as a "blessing" insofar as they make possible the offerings in the temple (2:14). Thus he gives a more pronounced liturgical flavor to the blessing which these foods were in themselves (Deut. 11:14–15). The final favorable response of the Lord (2:19) is also typical of what a prophet might proclaim at a liturgy. Despite all this, the prose notation of 2:18 indicates a passage of time difficult to associate with a particular liturgical ceremony and leaves us wondering, without final answer, whether Joel himself was directly involved in some liturgy as a prophet.

He also draws his inspiration from the prophet Amos, who had successfully begged the Lord to halt the effects of a threatening plague of locusts (Amos 7:1–3). Amos had spoken of the "day of the Lord" which would be directed in punishment against Israel (Amos 5:18–20). Joel borrows his imagery (Joel 2:1–2), but, remarkably enough, redirects its force. For him, the locust plague is an image of the coming day of the Lord when Israel will be defended from the final onslaught of its enemies. Here once more Deuteronomy provides Joel with a description which allows him to reshape the words of Amos. Deut. 7:21 spoke of the Lord himself as "great and awesome" in protecting Israel against its enemies, and Joel characterizes that coming day as likewise "great and awesome" (2:11). Thus he does not regard the locust plague as a punishment for sin, but rather as a summons to closer union with God in preparation for God's final salvation for his people. Surely Joel's appeal for conversion shares the Deuteronomic view that no man is without sin (1 Kings 8:46), but the accent is not on the guilt of Israel. There is no confession of sin in Joel, such as we find in Deuteronomic passages (e.g., 1 Kings 8:47). Joel will evoke the Deuteronomic theme of blessing (Joel 2:14), but he avoids the curse as punishment for sin. This is all the more striking when one observes how close Joel is to Deut. 28, a chapter which emphasizes the curses of punishment. In any case, the guilt of Israel is not stressed, for even the totally innocent are to partake in the fast (Joel 2:16), even as Josiah implored God through weeping and tearing his garments despite his own innocence (2 Kings 22:19; 23:25).

We may suspect that Joel's injunction not to tear one's garments is not a prohibition but rather a focusing on the interior character of conversion, an emphasis which may also in part explain his silence about animal sacrifice, so often decried by the preexilic prophets as an empty show. Thus Joel will not allow himself an easy understanding of God's providence, as if all disaster were a punishment for sin. He affirms God's final salvation of his people but leaves the interim stages in mystery (2:14).

Second Lesson: 2 Cor. 5:20b–6:2. Rarely does Paul speak of reconciliation, but it is a concept central to his thought, as well as to this passage. We can be aided in understanding him by referring to his more systematic presentation in Rom. 5, as well as to the interpretations in Col. 1 and Eph. 2–3, which are probably the work of his disciples.

Reconciliation is coupled with divine "wrath" (Rom. 5:9), a word which expresses man's fallen condition rather than an emotion of God. In fact, so far is God from anger that he does not need to be reconciled to man, but is himself the reconciler. Here Paul moves beyond the relationship of divine wrath and reconciliation as expressed in Jewish tradition (cf. 2 Macc. 5:20) and parallels rather the thought of Jesus who spoke of the reign of God as a totally new gift to be received by man (Matt. 5:3–9; cf. also 2 Cor. 5:17). Such an understanding helps clarify 2 Cor. 5:21, which is not to be interpreted as if God were exacting some form of punishment. Rather, it is a highly compressed reformulation of Isa. 53, concerning the suffering servant. It makes use of abstract language ("sin," "righteousness") which comes close to Paul's technique of making "sin" and "grace" characters in a type of morality play (Rom. 5:12–21). Comparison of 2 Cor. 5:21 with Gal. 3:13 and Rom. 8:3 further indicates that Paul understands the corporeal dimension of man as the source of his vulnerability and thus sees the death of Jesus as the death of man's weakness. Why this should be so, however, is not logically reasoned out by Paul but is presented as a manifestation of God's mysterious will to communicate his own holiness to man (2 Cor. 5:21), a gift as devoid of prior explanation as creation itself (2 Cor. 5:17).

For Paul, the meaning of the present moment is expressed through "reconciliation." He associates it with the word "now" (Rom. 5:11; 2 Cor. 6:2), as did his disciples later (Col. 1:22; Eph. 2:13). He stresses that moment still further by quoting his own imperative, "Be reconciled" (2 Cor. 5:20). In every present moment the message continues, and thus it remains a program for the future. Some have been reconciled already, but the whole world must be told of its reconciliation (2 Cor. 5:19; Rom. 11:15), as the generalized language of 2 Cor. 5:21 itself implies. That not even the inanimate world is to be excluded from the effects of this message is the understanding of Col. 1:20 and probably that of Paul himself (cf. Rom. 8:20–21).

The gift of reconciliation is specially linked to the death of Christ (Rom. 5:10). It allows this death to be more than a past moment of history and to be actually a divine force unleashed by God which enters into the being of the Christian himself. This bearing the death of Christ in oneself is preeminently true of Paul, for it is his calling as apostle to continue Christ's work through this power (2 Cor. 4:10–12), but it is true also for those who receive his message (Rom. 6:3–5; see also 2 Cor. 4:16–18). Reconciliation means thus a dying joined with possibility for a new life that is lived now and directed toward resurrection.

So central to his message and even his own being is the word of reconciliation that Paul determines his own identity in relation to it (2 Cor. 5:20; see also Col. 1:23 and Eph. 3:7). We may therefore conclude that in 2 Corinthians, where Paul is at such pains to defend his apostleship, he sees reconciliation to God as implying reconciliation of the community with Paul himself (2 Cor. 6:11–13).

Gospel: Matt. 6:1–6, 16–18 (19–21). These teachings of Jesus on almsgiving, prayer, and fasting have ancient roots that go even beyond the origins of Israel. Shortly before the time of Moses, an Egyptian document called "The Instruction of Ani" advised the reader to pray to God with words hidden in a loving heart and then God would respond to one's need.

Israelite wisdom continued in this tradition and provided the background for these words of Jesus. The ancient maxims spoke of how God could see all, good and evil, even the recesses of man's heart (Prov. 15:3; 21:2; 24:12); they taught that one should pray to God with few words (Eccles. 5:1–2); almsgiving, besides fostering the stability of society which made peaceful life possible, was also a special safeguard against future personal dangers and would surely be rewarded by God (Prov. 19:17; Tob. 4:9; Sir. 29:12). In fact, the promise of reward specially characterizes this literature, which sought to persuade its reader through the benefits true wisdom could bring (Prov. 22:4).

The man who was truly wise would be able to discern the proper time for the proper action, a task which Ecclesiastes finally judges was beyond man's ability (Eccles. 3:11); Jesus, however, brought the wisdom of man face-to-face with the urgent demand of the "final time," the goal of human history, for which the time had come (Matt. 16:2–3). Thus, timeless wisdom became directed to the moment of God's unique gift to man, a transformation expressed in the wisdom language of the beatitudes which now heralded God's reign (Matt. 5:3–10; see Prov. 3:13; 8:33–34; contrast Prov. 22:11 and Matt. 5:8). The Lord's Prayer (Matt. 6:9–13) points the words of our passage in this same direction and, as a community prayer, prevents too literal an interpretation of the command to pray in the privacy of one's room (Matt. 6:6). In fact, this latter instruction also emphasizes the approaching judgment by its allusion to Isa. 26:20. Similarly, the treasures built up by almsgiving had no clear reference to a future life in the OT texts cited above, but now they do (Matt. 6:4, 20–21). The maxim that one's heart can be found where his treasure is now becomes a warning not to risk total personal loss in the ensuing struggle (cf. Mark 8:36). Even fasting is transformed, now partaking of the preparations for a banquet (Matt. 6:17; see Luke 7:46), in this case, the heavenly banquet (Matt. 8:11). This focusing on the goal intended by God helps us to grasp the paradox of the individual's secret virtue and the open example of the community (Matt. 5:14–16).

Wisdom writers sometimes presented truth in contrasting aspects (Prov. 11:24; 13:23); in our present text, the contrast is between the secrecy and the revelation of the final days. If each one acts as God wills, then God's purpose will inevitably be achieved and the light shed by the community (Matt. 5:14) will be that of the glorified Jerusalem, the city set on a hill, giving light to all who come (Isa. 2:2–5). Thus when Jesus says the light of the disciples must shine before men (Matt. 5:16), his words are less an exhortation to give good example than a proclamation that God will inevitably achieve his goal: the city cannot be hidden (Matt. 5:14); the seed grows even if man does not know how (Mark 4:27–29); everything done in secret (man's prayer included) is bound to be revealed (Matt. 10:26).

The use of wisdom thought to announce God's future reign occurred in Jewish literature outside the Scriptures; it remained for Christian tradition to direct this thought specially to Christ. This Matthew did, to the point where Christ was presented as the very embodiment of God's wisdom (compare Luke 11:49 and Matt. 23:34; also Sir. 24:1–22 and Matt. 11:28–30). Thus, in our text, Wisdom himself speaks in language that suits well the situation of the church today, a community which needs wise teaching as a guide through its day-to-day living, but which needs as well to keep its eyes focused on the promised goal of history.

HOMILETICAL INTERPRETATION

Ash Wednesday is the church's point of entry onto the road which leads to Good Friday and Easter. The preacher should never lose sight of these goals as he sets out on his Lenten journey. The cross and resurrection are the pivot points of the entire Christian year, but they dominate in a special way this season which immediately precedes them. Every sermon must be worked out under the full light of what occurred at Golgotha and in Joseph's garden.

In the ancient church, Lent was an intensive period of preparation for Easter baptism. Catechumens were exposed once more to the great themes of the faith. Likewise, for the baptized, Lent was a time for the rehearsal of these themes, culminating in the renewal of baptismal vows at the Easter vigil. Hence, the lections for the Lenten Sundays were selected with special care. It was crucial that the history of salvation be recapitulated, that the centrality of repentance and faith be made clear, and that worshipers be led once more into a dying and rising with Christ.

The present "C Series" of lessons is in continuity with the ancient tradition. OT lessons offer such key pericopes as the patriarchal creed (the First Sunday in Lent), the call of Moses (the Third Sunday in Lent), and the "passion" of Jeremiah (the Second Sunday in Lent). The epistles also are notable for the solidity of their content. Luke, as has been the case throughout this cycle, provides the gospel readings, moving from the temptation story on the First Sunday to the parable of the wicked husbandman on the Fifth. It will help the preacher to catch the mood of this season and to plot out his homiletical course if he reads through all the lessons for Ash Wednesday and the Lenten Sundays.

What has been said thus far suggests that penitence is only one of the themes to be stressed during Lent. This whole season is not to be draped in black. On Ash Wednesday, however, the mood is decidedly somber. The church meets in "solemn assembly" (Joel 2:15). In former times, the rubbing of ashes on the forehead was accompanied by the sobering words, "Remember man, that you are dust." Both our mortality and our iniquity constitute our burden on this day.

All three lections for Ash Wednesday sound the call for a repentant church. It is one of those days when the lessons reinforce and supplement each other. It should be noted that these lections remain stable throughout the three cycles.

Ash Wednesday preaching offers an opportunity to deal with people's unspoken question, "Why *should* we repent?" Penitence must be seen as something other than morbid self-examination. Neither this day nor the season which follows is a time for spiritual pulse-taking or exercises in self-improvement. We repent because of the cross which stands at the

end of the Lenten pilgrimage. Penitence has its springs in the consciousness of the cost to God of our redemption. We recognize our wrongness
most plainly when we are struck by the hurt it inflicts upon others. Ash
Wednesday and Lent call us to reflect upon the hurt to God. Yet, we
must see that we inflict pain upon God chiefly by inflicting it upon each
other ("as you did it not to one of the least of these"; Matt. 25:45). One
task of the preacher, then, is to help us see the vertical dimension of all
the horizontal expressions of our sinfulness. Everything that separates us
from our neighbor, deprives him of good, or afflicts him with evil is to
be gathered into the cry of penitence, "Against thee, thee only have I
sinned" (Ps. 51:4a). And the cross is the point in human history at which
all the lines of human iniquity, including our own, converge visibly upon
God, only to be taken up into his unfathomable love.

First Lesson. To hear this pericope in its context and to catch the
sweep of Joel's majestic poetry, the preacher should read the whole of
this brief book. The images tumble over each other. Especially powerful
is the central one—the billowing, ravaging clouds of locusts. Is it a his-
toric pestilence Joel is describing, or are the locusts symbols of a ruthless
invading army? In either case, the striking visual quality of Joel's language is a worthy model for the contemporary preacher.

The exegesis calls attention to Joel's "profound love of community
worship." Though he wants internal reality to be consistent with external
practice, he doesn't dismiss liturgical rites out of hand. He is a cultic
prophet, or better, a prophetic cultist. That is, he retains his devotion to
the liturgical assembly even while he calls it to repentance. In short, his
stance is that of the parish pastor. We are to be at once fully committed
to the church and also sharply critical of that in its life which violates
God's purposes. God calls us into a "lover's quarrel" with his people, and
the collapse of either element in that paradoxical phrase tragically com-
promises our ministry. Especially on this day of penitence, it is important
that people sense we are preaching repentance with "tears in our hearts."

The interplay of the individual and the corporate is also notable in
this text. Though a change of heart such as that which Joel calls for must
obviously occur within persons, his sermons are addressed to the nation
as a whole. Few if any modern preachers have the ear of a whole nation. The body we address is the gathered congregation. Should our
appeal for repentance be pitched to individuals or to the community?
The prevailing tradition during Lent has been to spotlight the more

personal attitudes and private behavior patterns which separate us from God. Does Joel suggest that we focus instead upon the infidelities of which we are corporately guilty as God's people? Can we make Ash Wednesday a day for examining the nature of our response as a congregation to God's call to mission in the world? The NT reminds us that there is a time for "judgment to begin with the household of God" (1 Pet. 4:17).

Judgment, however, is set within the promise in this passage. Note the present tense in 2:13: "Return to the Lord, your God, for he *is* gracious and merciful." Repentance isn't a tit-for-tat transaction; repentance is possible only because God is already turned toward us before we even think to turn toward him.

Second Lesson. As the exegesis indicates, the key words in this passage are "reconcile" and "reconciliation." One of the problems facing the preacher is how to let these terms resound with the full force of their NT meaning. In common usage the word "reconcile" frequently has a rather passive connotation. A person "reconciles" himself to some harsh circumstance in his life, meaning that he grudgingly accepts it. Since there appears to be no possibility of altering it, he adopts a stoical "grin and bear it" attitude.

For Paul, the word "reconcile" has a far more positive, energetic thrust. It refers to God's aggressive action in setting right a relationship that has gone wrong. God doesn't merely endure man's alienation from himself in sin. Neither is it sufficient to say that God "accepts" us even though we're unacceptable to him (Tillich). Such language fails to communicate the utterly incredible initiative of grace by which God the wronged One acts to heal a relationship for whose brokenness we are responsible.

In order to give expression to this movement of grace, the preacher will find himself struggling for appropriate analogies. Hosea found such an analogy in his own tragic marriage. As often as Gomer deserted him for a life of open prostitution, Hosea searched her out in her degradation and restored her to his side. But no human symbol is adequate. In Christ, God does more than search for us. His reconciling act involves an exchange with us. In the crucified Christ, we see God taking upon himself the sin and death which properly belong to us. There are echoes here, as the exegesis suggests, of the great suffering servant song in Isa. 53. This Ash Wednesday epistle already foreshadows Good Friday, when it becomes plain that "he made him to be sin who knew no sin" (v. 21).

The clearest clues to the radicality of God's reconciling act should come from the life of the church and the biographies of Christians. This is the force of Paul's designation of himself and others as "ambassadors for Christ." Christians go forth into this broken world literally "representing" Christ's passion on its behalf. The life of the contemporary "body of Christ" and that of its members will reveal the stigmata—the marks of crucifixion. The credentials of Christ's envoys in the midst of an alien society are wounds.

"Bearing the death of Christ" (see exegesis) is the acid test of the integrity of the church. A congregation could center its Ash Wednesday self-examination around the question, Where are we, as the body of Christ in this time and place, letting God make "his appeal through us" (v. 20) by costly self-offering to the world?

Gospel. The trap awaiting the preacher in any text from the Sermon on the Mount is that of turning it into a new law. Because of their hortatory form, we are tempted to lay the proclamations of these chapters upon our people's backs as though they were rules to be obeyed. To do this is to crush them beneath a weight impossible to carry.

It helps if we approach the Sermon on the Mount not as a set of new laws but as a chain of illustrations of the new life in the new age. We are being shown what a man or woman living in the new age "looks like," or, as the case may be, does *not* look like. The Gospel for Ash Wednesday projects both a positive and a negative image of life in Christ, particularly as it manifests itself in specifically religious practices.

In most parishes, the arrival of Lent brings an acceleration of religious activities. Acts of devotion, extra occasions of worship, and special disciplines of prayer and charity are part of the tradition of "keeping Lent." There is nothing in this lesson which denies the validity of such practices. Jesus doesn't reject the time-honored pieties of his own day—i.e., almsgiving, praying, and fasting. He rather makes it clear on what basis any religious observances can be expressive of the new life he brings.

For Jesus, the key lies in the focus of acts of piety. They are consistent with the new life only if they home in without deviation upon their target. Prayer must move unswervingly to God. Charity must be aimed unerringly at the needy neighbor. The moment either is deflected from its course by any thought of self-justification or the praise of men, all is lost. Discipleship degenerates into hypocrisy (v. 2), the root meaning of which is "acting a part." As on the stage, a role other than that of the real self is assumed, and the applause of an audience becomes a primary goal. The drive for a straight line of consistency between motive and act links these sayings of Jesus with the note Joel has already sounded in the OT reading: "Rend your hearts and not your garments."

In this text, as throughout the sermon, Jesus can be preached as the embodiment of what he proclaims (see exegesis). He prayed, he fasted, he did good works. But he did all this without ostentation. He never "played to the galleries." His eye was always focused strictly on the target of his action—either God or the needy person. There were no sidelong glances toward an audience he hoped would admire and applaud. Thus, he *is* the new life here proclaimed, and the white light which shines from him upon us exposes how much enemy territory remains still to be conquered by the "new man" we are becoming in Christ.

The First Sunday in Lent

Lutheran	Roman Catholic	Episcopal	Presbyterian and UCC
Deut. 26:5–10	Deut. 26:4–10	Deut. 26:5–10	Deut. 26:5–11
Rom. 10:8b–13	Rom. 10:8–13	James 1:12–18	Rom. 10:8–13
Luke 4:1–13	Luke 4:1–13	Luke 4:1–13	Luke 4:1–13

EXEGESIS

First Lesson: Deut. 26:5–10. This profession of faith was to be recited by the worshiping Israelite when he offered the first fruits of his crops in the presence of a priest in the Jerusalem temple (Deut. 26:1–3). The circumstances of the offering remain obscure. There is no mention of a particular festival at which this was to be done; it is further puzzling how one could be expected to bring a portion of all the crops (v. 2); they would be harvested at different times and would necessitate several trips to Jerusalem, which, by the time of Deuteronomy, was the only legitimate center of worship. Perhaps the three festivals in Deut. 16 are the appropriate time, but this is not clear. Obviously our author is less interested in clarifying ritual prescriptions than in expressing the spirit which should motivate religious practice. Thus he presents a brief summary of sacred history (vv. 5–9), the like of which could serve elsewhere for a variety of homiletic and catechetic purposes (cf. Deut. 6:21–24; Josh. 24:2–13; 1 Sam. 12:8–12); here he transforms it into a prayer by appending the conclusion (v. 10). Such an interest in personal prayer is elsewhere manifest in Deuteronomic writings, where key summaries of theology were cast in a prayer form (e.g., 2 Sam. 7:18–29; 1 Kings 8:23–53).

The recipient of God's blessings throughout the prayer is the people of Israel, now even called a "nation" (v. 5), a title suggesting the status of Israel as an international power (cf. Deut. 4:6, 7, 8, 34), but the prayer concludes focusing on the gratitude of the individual person, who has internalized the history as his own and offers his own response (v. 10). The author is careful to highlight the personal character of the relationship between God and man. God "sees" and "hears" (v. 7); he acts directly, apart from the mediating angel of the older tradition (Num. 20:15–16). The prayer quality of the text is heightened further by its echoing the language and pattern of several psalms (Pss. 30, 34, 116). A contemporary of our author, the prophet Jeremiah, himself creatively adapted similar psalm language to express the depths of his personal anguish (e.g., Jer. 15:10–21; 20:7–13); in our passage, the nation is the focus, but Jeremiah's concern for personal, heartfelt worship is also expressed. Indeed, the whole of Deut. 26 is structured to suggest a personal dialogue between God and man; God's past faithfulness is reviewed (vv. 5–10); man presents his own faithfulness as a plea for further blessing (vv. 13–15); both God and man agree to accept each other (vv. 17–18). In the whole chapter the prayerful tone of psalm language is present; the thanksgiving for deliverance (vv. 5–10) and the protestations of innocence (vv. 13–14) echo a similar sequence in Ps. 18.

Israel may be a "nation" like others, but it is specially God's own people (Deut. 26:18); similarly, it may enjoy the fruits of the earth as people everywhere do, but these crops are to be seen as the sign of the unique love which God has shown Israel and which he now offers to each one who shares the fruit of the land. The history of the people is meant to touch the heart of each person. According to Deuteronomy, it was even so at the time of the original event. The "great terror" accompanying the exodus (v. 8) is the response of Israel, a reverence for God quite other than a paralyzing fear. Such devout "fear" rises from a heart which God alone can fathom; the events of the exodus are God's "test" for Israel, bringing forth from the heart of each one the sentiments that lie hidden there (cf. especially Exod. 20:20; also Exod. 15:25; 16:4; Deut. 13:3; Jer. 17:9–10; Prov. 16:2; 23:17; cf. Prov. 1:7 and 14:33). The Israelite of every age is meant to share that "fear," which is really a wholehearted love of God (cf. 1 Sam. 12:24; Deut. 6:2, 4), the spirit which animates all the laws in Deuteronomy. Our text fits especially well in the closing chapter of the legislation, for it expresses the successful result of the "testing," the gratitude of a heart willing to observe what the Lord has commanded (cf. Deut. 8:2).

Second Lesson: Rom. 10:8b–13. The Israelite quest for wisdom could lead to contrasting results: a sense of exhilaration at man's cultural achievements (e.g., 1 Kings 5:9–14) but also an awareness of how futile was man's quest for full understanding (e.g., Prov. 16:1, 9; 20:24). Israel came to appreciate its law in relationship to such unattainable wisdom: mysterious as wisdom might be, nonetheless, its quintessence has been given in the law, the guide by which a man may wisely order his life (cf. Bar. 3:37–4:1; Eccles. 12:12–14; Sir. 24:22). Perhaps the earliest such understanding of the law is found in the passage which forms the background for our present text in Paul, Deut. 30:11–14, in which Moses proclaims that the impossible journey up to the sky or across the sea in search of wisdom is not necessary, since it is nearby in the word of the law. By the time of the NT, such an understanding could be modified to the extent that Jesus was seen as the source of wisdom, offering a new interpretation of the law which eased the burdens caused by the strict interpretations of some Pharisees (Matt. 11:28–30). But Paul's interpretation is more radical. For him, Jesus does not revivify the law, but rather introduces an entirely new principle of salvation. The words of Moses in Deuteronomy are actually used against him, as the "word" of the law in Deut. 30:14 is transformed by Paul into the "word" of Christian preaching (Rom. 10:8), which is the action of Christ himself (Rom. 10:17).

In transforming the meaning of Moses' words, Paul makes a further adaptation of the wisdom tradition. In Rom. 10:5, Moses writes of a holiness based on law, but in v. 6, someone other than Moses speaks. Here we are close to the OT figure of personified Wisdom speaking to men (Prov. 8:1–10), but now Wisdom is transformed into a Christian figure, the new holiness or "righteousness" itself. We are approaching the thought of John, who presented Christ as revealing himself even in the words of the OT (John 5:46; 8:56).

Before we consider the actual text chosen for the liturgy, our background observations should take special note of the first two parentheses which Paul inserts into his quotation from Deut. 30:11–14 (cf. Rom. 10:6–7). They are best understood as a reference to the ascension and glorification of Jesus (v. 6) and also to his resurrection from the dead (v. 7). They are particularly valuable to Paul as marking the outer limits of the "journey" that Jesus has "traveled," the heights of heaven and the nether world of the dead. In order to have the OT text express this bipolarity, Paul has transformed Deuteronomy's journey across the sea into a journey to the nether world.

As for Rom. 10:8*b*–13 itself, these same two parentheses discussed above are related to the two primitive professions of faith in v. 9. The first question (v. 6) corresponds to the confession "Jesus is Lord," whereas the second (v. 7) parallels the belief "God raised him from the dead." Further, it is probable that these two professions had different origins, in Gentile and Jewish communities respectively. Paul, by preserving their primitive form and yet blending them both into the faith experience of a single individual, is consciously giving expression to the removal of distinction between Jew and Greek (v. 12).

The notion was traditional in wisdom thought that the lips express what is truly in the heart (Prov. 22:18; 23:15–16; 24:1–2); thus confession with the lips and belief in the heart can be regarded as deriving from basically the same experience of sanctification. Their unusual sequence in v. 9, with confession preceding belief, is due to an imitation of the sequence in v. 8, which in turn follows Deut. 30:14. "Salvation" (v. 10) is a fuller development of "justification." This latter describes man's present state, whereas "salvation" for Paul is directed to future fulfillment (see especially Rom. 5:9). Thus, in the letters of Paul most widely accepted as authentic (excluding the Pastorals, Colossians, and Ephesians), he allows some experience of "salvation" in the present time (1 Cor. 1:18; 15:2), but even in these passages as in all others concerning "salvation," the context makes clear the direction toward final resurrection. Only once does Paul say "we *have been* saved" (Rom. 8:24), but he hastens to add "by hope"!

Confession on the lips is closely associated with Jesus' title of "Lord" (vv. 9, 13), giving evidence of how Jesus had become central to the liturgy as the Father was in the OT (compare v. 13 and Joel 2:32, in some Bibles printed as Joel 3:5). The link between this profession and "salvation" points up the liturgy as a source for sustaining hope in the final resurrection.

Gospel: Luke 4:1–13. Jesus enters the desert under the influence of the Holy Spirit, who, in Luke, is especially associated with the gift of wisdom (cf. Luke 4:22 and Prov. 16:21, 23; see also Acts 6:3, 10). In keeping with the wisdom concern of this passage, the encounter between Jesus and the devil recalls the testing of Job by Satan, except that the devil in Luke is not a member of the divine court as in Job. In the gospel, the devil seeks to draw forth how Jesus understands his sonship, recently proclaimed at his baptism (Luke 3:22), somewhat as Satan sought to draw forth from Job any rebellion that may have been deep in his heart.

Again in harmony with the wisdom setting, the meeting of Jesus and the devil is something like a rabbinic disputation about the true nature of messiahship. The parties in the debate marshal their arguments from Scripture. The devil makes use of Ps. 91:11–12 (Luke 4:10–11), and with good precedent, since Ps. 91:13 is probably the basis of the Marcan temptation scene (Mark 1:13). If Jesus will seek signs of God's providence, the devil knows he need not fear him. But all three responses of Jesus to the devil say in effect that he will not seek miraculous protection for himself; he will not be like false messiahs whose understanding was merely human. Each time, Jesus answers with a quote from Deuteronomy, itself a book expressive of wisdom given by God (Deut. 4:5–6). Each response of Jesus reveals an attitude which is the mark of a wise man, total submission to God's plan (cf. Prov. 16:3, 9; 19:21; 21:30).

The temptation foreshadows the formation of a new community, in that Jesus embodies within himself the history of his people and remains faithful in those situations in which they failed. Jesus relives the experience of the people who had just come through the waters of the exodus and were subjected to a series of tests so that God might bring forth their true sentiments (cf. Exod. 15:2–17:7, especially 16:4).

The result of the testing is that the devil leaves Jesus, apparently having learned that this man's understanding of messiahship is different from that of other men. Jesus is a threat and will have to be openly attacked. The devil returns around the time of the passion, this time looking for a weakness in Jesus' companions (Luke 22:31) and finding that he can take possession of Judas (Luke 22:3). Jesus once more faces a testing, this time in the garden (Luke 22:40, 46); it is for this far more bitter scene that Luke reserves the comfort afforded by the angel (Luke 22:43), after omitting it from the temptation in the desert (contrast Mark 1:13; Matt. 4:11). But Jesus remains faithful to his initial stand in the desert. Here he speaks openly of his trials in which his disciples now share (Luke 22:28); he insists that the authority of earthly kings is to have no place among his own followers (Luke 22:25–26), much as he had rejected the power and glory of the devil's offer (Luke 4:6–8). For Luke, the disciples of Jesus must share in his work of serving (Luke 22:26). The new people whose existence was hinted at in the desert now receives its mandate from Jesus, and it is for various forms of service that his disciples will receive the same Spirit that guided Jesus in the desert (cf. Acts 6:2, 4). This new community can see itself symbolically present with Jesus in the desert, particularly insofar as at the time of Luke, it had to endure the earthly power of Roman persecution without miraculous signs of God's deliverance.

"When a man is wise to his people's advantage, the fruits of his knowledge are enduring" (Sir. 37:22, NAB).

HOMILETICAL INTERPRETATION

The connections among the three lessons for the First Sunday in Lent are not immediately obvious. Each of the texts can speak with a clear voice of its own; yet, as they are explored in concert, some interrelationships begin to emerge. For instance, both the First Lesson and the Second Lesson include confessions of faith. And some will see the Deuteronomic recital of old Israel's formative history partially recapitulated in the triumph of Jesus (the head of new Israel) in the wilderness—a pattern which is to be traced again by his body, the church.

First Lesson. As the exegetical notes on this passage make clear, we are dealing with liturgical material. The setting for the formulary words in these verses is the ancient Israelite festival, at which time the faithful brought to the sanctuary the first fruits of the land. A homiletical key to this material may lie in the recognition that we are dealing with a liturgy both of *recollection* and *dedication*.

This duality is signaled by the abrupt shift in linguistic form (see exegesis) which takes place in v. 10. Vv. 5–8 are cast in the form of creedlike recital. God's mighty acts in the past, beginning with the patriarch Jacob and running through the exodus to the promised land, are remembered. But God is not addressed directly. Suddenly, in v. 10, the worshiper is forced out of his stance of rehearsing the past and enters himself into present dialogue with God. He addresses God directly. An

"I-Thou" dimension is introduced into the liturgy. In the light of what God has done in his people's history, the worshiper now performs his own act of commitment.

Preaching throughout Lent, and specifically with respect to this text, should have this same bifocal concern. Certainly there needs to be a stress on *recollection*, or remembrance. Contemporary American life is notable for its "history-lessness." We live in the "now generation," whose relationships and loyalties are chiefly horizontal. Verticality, with its sense of deep-rootedness in a rich tradition, is not easily maintained. American Christianity shares this general cultural problem. We become so absorbed in the present chapter of the church's story that we easily neglect the recollection of those crucial events in past chapters which have formed us into the people of God. Each Sunday the recital of the creed, especially the second article, is an aid to such remembrance. This lection from Deuteronomy reminds us that our roots go deeper still. Ancient Israel's story is our story, too, and we begin to understand our true identity only as we hold in consciousness this "rock from whence we are hewn."

But recollection is not an end itself. It is the prelude, as in the liturgical text of this lection, to *dedication*. We recite the story of our past preparatory to adding our own chapters to that story in the present. "Remembrance of things past" is the time of rehearsal; there comes the moment, then, when we must step on stage and become ourselves participants in the drama. Memory and commitment are the alternating thrusts which drive the people of God in their life and mission in the world.

One of the "troubles with the church" is the fact that, forgetful of its own true story, it has allowed other stories, other histories to determine its existence. It may be the story of the nation, resulting in a Christianity which confuses faith with patriotism and sees the church only as a bulwark of the state. Then the church "blesses the bombs," i.e., gives blind endorsement to every national policy. Or, we may let the mythology of race determine our existence. The "Nazi church" in Hitler's Germany is an example, as is every congregation which has insisted on remaining a one-color enclave. All forms of "culture Christianity" are symptoms of the loss of our roots in our distinctive history, signs of our refusal to be shaped by the crucial events of our own past.

This Deuteronomic text affords the preacher the opportunity to forge again his people's identity by rehearsing with them the formative moments of their history and to call them to "become what they are" in the present crisis. All of this is consistent with the traditional understanding of Lent as a time for renewing the vows of our baptism, the point at which our own biographies are incorporated into that history which stretches from the patriarchs through Jesus to ourselves.

Second Lesson. A complicating feature of this text for preaching lies in the fact that it is itself the interpretation of still another text. Paul quotes portions of Deut. 30:11–14 (see exegesis) and makes of them direct references to the gospel. The preacher today, however, need not follow all the twists and turns of Paul's exegesis in shaping his own sermon. Paul's essential message is clear as light. His essential word in this pericope, as throughout Romans, is simply this: *justification is by faith, not works.*

This message stands out more starkly if vv. 5–7 are added to the appointed lesson. Here the righteousness, or justification, which comes by faith is contrasted with that which men try to obtain by "law," i.e., by every attempt at self-justification. This text provides the preacher an opportunity to expose all our illusory efforts to find a way of removing the radical question which hangs over our existence. Paul puts it in terms of vain efforts to "ascend into heaven" or to plumb "the abyss." In our own preaching, we will need to speak of the contemporary expressions of this perennial human quest: the ways we shore up our egos with symbols of achievement or affluence, the resurgent interest in the magical and occult, the attempt to prove our maturity by flaunting our freedom, or, conversely, by adhering to rigid disciplines. These are all attempts to take the question of our salvation into our own hands. Tragically, we discover that, despite all our struggling, the question mark remains.

But exposure of the futility of all our human efforts to deal with the ultimate question of our existence is only the beginning of the preacher's work with this text. The central task is to proclaim what Paul calls "the word of faith." This is his shorthand definition of the act of grace from God's side which bridges the chasm we cannot cross from our side. Paul uses the time-honored vocabulary of the Christian tradition, e.g., "the righteousness based on faith" (v. 6), and the belief by which we are "justified" (v. 10). Most congregations today will not find such language immediately accessible. Or, it may be so familiar as to have lost its potency. The preacher is under obligation, therefore, to search for contemporary words and images which will point unerringly to the reality of the same grace/faith relationship to which Paul's language witnesses. Tillich tried translating "justification by faith" into categories drawn from depth psychology, i.e., "accepting the fact that you are accepted though unacceptable." Others have found helpful, though imperfect, analogies in the interrelationships of marriage and family.

An important human consequence of "the righteousness based on faith" is drawn in vv. 11 and 12. Paul calls attention to the universality of the gospel of grace. There is "no distinction" among the various classifications of men who hear it. In his day, the highest dividing wall stood between "Jew and Greek." Today, depending upon the preaching context, it will be possible to show where walls arise between races and classes of many varieties. The "word of faith" demolishes all such barriers. Those on either side are one in sin and guilt; they are also one in the grace which accepts and overcomes that sin and guilt. Nothing so quickly levels the ground on which we stand with each other as the recognition of a common need and the reception of a common gift. "We are all beggars" (Luther), and we all receive from the same donor. In an age which is almost obsessive in its search for human community, this text can generate a sermon which declares the radical basis for community in Christ.

It would also be possible to build a sermon around the confession "Jesus is Lord," in v. 9. There are those who identify these three words as the most primitive form of the Christian creed. What does it mean to call Jesus "Lord" in the midst of the forces and structures in contemporary life which likewise lay claim to our allegiance? The OT lesson, with its ancient Israelite creed, presses us, as noted above, toward a similar question. To confess publicly "Jesus is Lord" forces us at once into a situation of conflict with the competing "lords" of the modern world. It also places us in the service of One who gives all that he demands.

Gospel. Early in his work with this text, the preacher will need to settle for himself how he is reading it. Is it a sober, factual account of a discrete event in Jesus' life? Or is it a symbol-crammed depiction of Jesus' unremitting battle with forces alien to his mission? Clues that it is the latter are to be found in the use of the "forty days" formula (as old Israel was "forty years" in the wilderness, so the head of new Israel is "forty days" there) and in the stylized nature of the three tests. It will, in general, be neither wise nor necessary to drag this question of historicity into the pulpit, but the way the preacher resolves it for himself will condition the way he preaches from this text. Certainly a recognition of its mythic elements in no way diminishes its potency as a bearer of truth.

Broadly speaking, there are two possible preaching approaches to this pericope. The first would be to concentrate on its formal aspects, i.e., what the bare fact of Jesus' temptations—independent of their substance —speaks to us. The temptation narrative is of a piece with the passion narrative in dramatically revealing Jesus' oneness with us in our humanity. His unique vocation, his ultimate origin and destiny did nothing to exempt him from our common lot. Not only did he enter with us into pain and death, as we will remember again during Holy Week; already at the beginning of Lent this lesson recalls to us his total identification with us in the full range of what it means to be man. To be human is to be tested. Whatever else we confess about him, we must not undercut the acknowledgment that he was "bone of our bone and flesh of our flesh." Other parts of the NT make appropriate theological comments on what it means that God in Christ participates with us in the depths of our existence (cf. Phil. 2:6; Heb. 2:18; 4:15, 16; 5:8).

All three evangelists heighten the drama of Jesus' descent into the arena of temptation by placing this symbolic narrative immediately on the heels of his baptism. He goes from the exaltation of the event in which his vocation is confirmed into the awesome struggle in the wilderness. Here is a rhythm familiar in our human experience. Heights are followed by depths. The clear centeredness of faith alternates with the confusions of doubt. The way of faithfulness to God's call was no less clouded with uncertainties for him than for us. Both this temptation story and the later account of his agony in Gethsemane establish the fact that for Jesus, as for us, the knowing and the doing of God's will precipitate violent struggles of the soul. But it is also made clear that other powers are always present in the darkness (cf. Luke 4:14; 22:43).

The second broad preaching approach to this text would be to focus on the substance of the paradigmatic temptations here presented. Basically, they reveal a two-pronged assault. On the one hand, Jesus was tempted to doubt his identity. Each test begins with the insinuating whisper, "If you are the Son of God . . ." On the other hand, Jesus was tempted to resort to shortcuts in fulfilling his vocation. Each of the tests forces into his consciousness an option other than the hard road of suffering love. Here, too, we see Jesus' oneness with us in our humanity, for it is precisely at these points that we are tempted. To doubt our identity as God's sons and daughters and to try to bypass the way of the cross are constant counterforces to the life of faith. The task of the preacher will be to make concrete the contemporary forms in which these testings come and to point convincingly to the grace which assists us in the midst of them.

The Second Sunday in Lent

Lutheran	Roman Catholic	Episcopal	Presbyterian and UCC
Jer. 26:8–15	Gen. 15:5–12, 17–18	Ezek. 36:22–28	Gen. 15:5–12, 17–18
Phil. 3:17–4:1	Phil. 3:17–4:1	1 Cor. 10:1–13	Phil. 3:17–4:1
Luke 13:31–35	Luke 9:28b–36	Mark 10:32–45	Luke 9:28–36

EXEGESIS

First Lesson: Jer. 26:8–15. Jeremiah has just delivered an address calling for religious reform. It is only a few short months since the tragic death of the great reformer-king Josiah; Jeremiah already sees, early in the reign of the new king Jehoiakim, that the only partially successful reform of Josiah is collapsing. A lengthy version of Jeremiah's sermon is found in chap. 7; in our chapter it is summarized in vv. 4–6. Thus we note here a lesser concern with the words of Jeremiah and a concentration rather on his person and the challenge to his role as a prophet. Jeremiah's response to the challenge (26:12–15) emphasizes the genuine character of his vocation, for he begins and ends his defense with the insistence that "it was the Lord who sent me." This interest in the person of Jeremiah is characteristic of the book as a whole; so numerous are the biographical episodes that the life of the prophet has actually become part of his message. Such thought eventually issued in the conviction that the prophet must actually give up his life for the sake of his message (cf. Luke 11:49–51). However, despite the focus on Jeremiah himself, his task assumes a prominence of its own. Jeremiah is not glorified here; even his self-defense becomes transformed into a further plea that his hearers reform their lives (26:13).

This restrained reverence for Jeremiah is usually attributed to the well-trained authorship of Jeremiah's friend, the scribe Baruch. As one schooled in court diplomacy, Baruch wrote with a style reminiscent of the covenant vocabulary in Deuteronomic passages (cf. Deut. 4:2 and Jer. 26:2). Thus Jeremiah's resignation to his fate echoes the covenant language attributed to the Gibeonites as they negotiated about a treaty they had just made (cf. Jer. 26:14 and Josh. 9:25). Also, the conditional "if" found so often in the laws of Deuteronomy characterizes Jeremiah's few words here (26:4, 15). The "perhaps" in God's word to Jeremiah (26:3) does not occur in Deuteronomy; this word accents the sovereignty and mystery of God's action as well as hopefulness in the midst of a threatening situation (cf. also 36:3, where Jeremiah retains this "perhaps" in a more desperate situation four years later). The use of treaty language suggests that the covenant which King Josiah had renewed (2 Kings 23:1–3) now lives on in the person of Jeremiah, who will eventually stand alone against his enemies, supported by promises of God's protection such as would ordinarily have been addressed to a king against a menacing foe (Jer. 1:18; 15:20).

There is no condition or "perhaps" in the charge against Jeremiah: he must be put to death (v. 8). To prophesy the destruction of the temple and city is construed as speaking against God himself, a crime punishable by death (1 Kings 21:13; Lev. 24:10–16). Shortly afterwards, Ezekiel would express the belief that the glory of God was separable from the temple (Ezek. 10); probably after the destruction itself, the Deuteronomic theologian would express a similar idea (1 Kings 8:27) and even allude to Jeremiah's prophecy (2 Kings 23:27). Jeremiah's own supporting argument is drawn from the destruction of the sanctuary at Shilo (v. 6), but he does add that putting him to death will only increase the crimes for which he had just said the temple and city must be destroyed (v. 15; cf. 7:6). This "shedding of innocent blood" no doubt refers to actual murder (Deut. 19:13); it includes also the offering of children in sacrifice (Ps. 106:38; Jer. 7:31) and the manipulating of legal process which deprives the poor of their livelihood (Ps. 94:6, 20–21; Jer. 7:6; 22:16–17). In the appraisal of the Deuteronomic theologian, it was such "bloodshed" which eventually did cause Jerusalem's destruction (2 Kings 21:16; 24:4).

We are beginning a most bitter period of Jeremiah's career. He is not yet isolated, for he can count on the support of the princes and several elders (26:16–19). Even the people appear to be on his side (26:16), but we detect that Jeremiah cannot rely on them (26:24), much as Jesus had to beware of people who believed in him but would not yet have been able to understand the words which he had just spoken against the temple (John 2:18–25).

Second Lesson: Phil. 3:17–4:1. This letter of Paul is especially renowned for its passage about the heights and depths traversed by Christ in his work of salvation (preexistence in heaven, descent to earth, return to glory), 2:6–11. This doctrine becomes a model for the humility of Christians, leading to a sharing in community which Paul announces as a major theme in this letter (1:5, 7). The rays of this teaching pervade chap. 3, where what had been said of Christ in chap. 2 is now reflected in the life of Paul and applied to the lives of the faithful: like Christ, Paul made no claims based on what had already been (cf. 2:6 and 3:7); further, our lowly body partakes of the lowliness of Christ (2:8; 3:21); the universal lordship of Christ will allow him to give us life (2:10–11; 3:18); the theme of "citizenship in heaven" (3:20) could indeed have particular force in Philippi, where the benefits of Roman citizenship were so highly prized (Acts 16:21, 37–38), but, more important still, it allows as close a union as possible with Christ's own descent into this "foreign" world (Phil. 2:7; see also 2:15).

This association with Christ notwithstanding, Paul still insists that its culmination lies in the future. Paul repeats that he has not yet reached the goal (3:12, 13) and claims that no degree of perfection exempts one from further progress (3:16). Even Paul's loving address to the community as "my joy and my crown" (4:1) suggests the victory that still lies in the future (1 Thess. 2:19). Some of the community may think otherwise (Phil. 3:15). Apparently they are being influenced by those enemies whose teaching includes laws about food ("belly") and circumcision ("shame"), 3:19. Who they are is not clear, but similar language about false teachers in Rom. 16:17–18 makes it likely they are not Jews but Christians. Perhaps they are a group that propose a doctrine of the spiritually elite, believers who have already reached the goal and consider regulations adapted from Judaism as signs of their superior status. Possibly they are forerunners of those against whom the pastoral epistles would later be directed (2 Tim. 2:18; 1 Tim. 4:1–3; Titus 1:10, 15).

Against such ideas Paul affirms that he wants to know the power of Christ's resurrection, but not without having his life patterned on the death of Christ (3:10). He invites the Philippians to imitate him in this (3:17) with an imitation that is obviously not a mere copying, but an entering into a new dimension of existence marked out by chaps. 2 and 3. Knowing the power of the resurrection is in this letter particularly expressed through the word "joy," a theme which constantly recurs. It is a sharing in the final victory even now and can break forth even if Paul must give up his life (2:17). It would be particularly intense for Paul if only the community will be united (2:2). Paul can experience joy even in the midst of tears (3:18). He may well affirm his independence (4:11), but his joy and tears depend on others; even here we may see Paul's share in the weakness assumed by Christ (2:7).

In a letter which stresses the humiliation and exaltation of Christ as well as the harmony of the community, we can well expect similarities to the Gospel of John. Especially striking is the theme of Christ in glory performing the work of God (Phil. 2:13; 3:21), more fully developed in John 5. Perhaps richest of all associations is in the theme of joy, which is felt by the Baptist even though he knows he must decrease (John 3:29–30), which is perfected in the community if they will love one another after the model of Christ (John 15:10–11), and which is the sign of a community who know that Christ has gone back to the Father (John 14:28).

Gospel: Luke 13:31–35. This passage is of particular interest for its varying approaches to understanding Christ. First, Jesus is a prophet (v. 33); he was no doubt seen as such by many during his own lifetime (cf. Mark 14:65; Luke 24:19). Another primitive conception appears, that of a "three-day" period referring to his earthly ministry rather than to the time between his death and resurrection. This is a concrete Semitic expression meaning "a short time" and containing here a nuance of God's special protection throughout that brief period. During these "three days," Jesus "goes his way" unharmed (v. 33); this theme had already appeared at the start of his ministry (4:30) as Jesus "went his way" through the hostile crowd; it will recur towards the end when the Son of man "goes his way" (22:22). This latter text brings out clearly the culmination of Jesus' journey at Calvary, a goal already before his eyes in our present passage (13:33). We are close to the Johannine concept of the "hour" of Jesus: nothing can happen to the Son until his hour comes (John 7:30). The roots of such theology appear in Ps. 91 and also in various passages in wisdom literature which either depict God as directing the steps of man's life (e.g., Prov. 16:9; Sir. 33:10–11) or else present divine Wisdom as protecting the chosen ones of God during the course of history (Wisd. of Sol. 10).

This providence has its negative side, however, for divine Wisdom also sends out prophets to their death (Luke 11:49), and such a mission has occurred with sufficient frequency to allow the martyrdom of prophets to become a proverbial pattern in history (13:33). Wisdom will nonetheless have its way, for it teaches that man's evil brings its own punishment (Prov. 26:27; 28:10); if Jerusalem rejects God's offer (Luke 13:34), it will in turn be abandoned by God (v. 35: cf. Prov. 1:31). Not even the craftiness of Herod the "fox" (v. 32) can oppose the wise plan of God. When he finally does encounter Jesus, the latter's silence before him will mark out Herod as merely a fool (Luke 23:9; cf. Prov. 23:9).

Our consideration of Jesus thus far has marked him out as a prophet, an emissary of divine Wisdom (Luke 11:49). But Luke also makes different use of a passage in which Wisdom herself speaks as the one who had repeatedly sent prophets to Israel. This brief section (vv. 34–35) echoes various OT passages about personified Wisdom: as here, Wisdom had previously offered herself and been rejected, then to withdraw in punishment (Prov. 1:24–28); the feminine personification of Wisdom (e.g., Prov. 8; Sir. 24) is preserved here in the image of Wisdom as the mother bird (Luke 13:34), a modification of the imagery in Ps. 91:4 and Isa. 31:5. Implicit in the gathering under Wisdom's wings is probably the gathering together of the faithful ones in the final age (Luke 13:29). This theology of Wisdom is best regarded as the work of Christian "wise men" who wrote after the destruction of the Jerusalem temple (A.D. 70) and interpreted it as God's judgment against Jerusalem for her repeated rejection of the prophets and finally of Jesus (see Luke 11:51).

Why Luke would have Jesus speak the words of personified Wisdom and yet refrain from identifying Jesus and Wisdom remains a problem for which tentative and partial solutions can be suggested. Luke may have avoided such an identification in order to provide room for his developing doctrine of the Holy Spirit, who is closely linked with Wisdom (cf. commentary on Luke 4:1–13 from last Sunday). Also, Luke may have been reacting against theological currents based on a type of wisdom which diminished the value of the human life of Jesus, particularly its culmination on the cross. Against such antihistorical thinking, Luke emphasized the genuine humanity of Jesus by reshaping the history of abstract Wisdom into the concrete human life of Christ and by linking it here closely with the "three-day" ministry of Jesus, a ministry of power (13:32), but a ministry not to be separated from its historical culmination on the cross (13:33).

HOMILETICAL INTERPRETATION

A clearly visible thread binds together the First Lesson and the Gospel for this Sunday. To state the theme most broadly, both reveal how the world normally reacts when God addresses it with his word. The entrance of God into human life is apt to evoke hostility rather than acceptance. We're more inclined to reject God's overture than to respond to it. This is so because his coming always sets in motion currents which run counter to the prevailing ones in any society. He will not, because he cannot, fit himself into our *status quo*. Salvation, personal or social, always involves a radical rearrangement of "the way things are." And because we usually have so much at stake in the established patterns and structures, we strike out against anything which threatens to alter them.

The First Lesson exhibits this general theme by way of an incident in the ministry of the prophet Jeremiah. Seen in the light of Lent and under the shadow of the cross, Jeremiah becomes an OT prototype of *the* prophet, Jesus of Nazareth. In today's Gospel, we see Jesus *en route* to his passion, flinging down the gauntlet in the heart of the stronghold of his opponents. It will be possible for the preacher to make either of these pericopes the basis for a sermon, using the other to illuminate his theme. Or he may find himself weaving the two together, remembering that the rejected One of whom the Gospel speaks is "God with us," thus bringing the overture of grace to our world to its crescendo and deepening the tragedy of rejection. The relationship of the Second Lesson to the other two lessons, as is so often the case, is not immediate, though it shares with them a mood of judgment.

The traditional title for this Second Sunday in Lent is "Reminiscere." The designation comes from the opening word of the Latin introit: "Remember, O Lord, thy tender mercies and thy lovingkindness: for they have been ever of old." It is the prayer of a servant of God beleaguered by his enemies, and, appropriate to the experience of Jeremiah, Jesus, and all who suffer because of their fidelity to the word, continues: "Let not mine enemies triumph over me: redeem Israel, O God, out of all his troubles."

First Lesson. It may be helpful to look first not directly at the possible content for a sermon on this text but rather at the model it proposes for one aspect of our work as preachers. This episode from Jeremiah's ministry raises the whole issue of "prophetic preaching." Usually we understand that phrase to mean preaching which confronts head on some public issue, or which calls the people of God sharply to account for their betrayal of their identity and mission. This pericope describes a classic instance of such preaching. In order to bring the whole incident vividly into view, chap. 26 should be read in its entirety.

Parallels with Jesus' own "prophetic" ministry are clear. Jesus' confrontation with the establishment, both religious and political, was the precipitating cause of his execution. Like Jeremiah, he carried his message, of which he refused to "hold back a word" (v. 2), straight into the citadel of his enemies. The word of truth demands to be delivered at the risk of the messenger's own safety—a fact which "prophets" down to our own day have learned in tragic ways (e.g., Dietrich Bonhoeffer and Martin Luther King.)

The specific ways in which the word will "afflict the comfortable" (as well as "comfort the afflicted") through our preaching today will vary with the configurations of life in each congregation and community. The preacher needs to be an expert and accurate diagnostician of sin in its personal and corporate dimensions, and must be prepared to have his diagnosis resisted. But he must also know himself to be a person under judgment. Then his "prophetic" word will be neither a denunciation from a lofty eminence nor a venting of private aggressions. It will be carried to his people out of agony over the hurt which must precede healing.

The substance of Jeremiah's message in this text is the attack on the illusion that identification with the institutions and rites of religion secures one in automatic privileges and absolves one from moral judgment. Jeremiah's target was a seventh century B.C. form of Bonhoeffer's "cheap grace"—a claiming of God's promise with no consequent acceptance of "the cost of discipleship."

This illusion, in its contemporary form, issues in "clubby" churchmanship which allows members to enjoy each other's fellowship while ignoring or rejecting people whose racial or cultural marks are different. It results in the success syndrome which leads a congregation to concentrate on its own institutional well-being at the expense of ministry to its surrounding community. It manifests itself in a careful avoidance of engagement with public issues which might stir controversy. A church equipment catalogue once carried this ad which unconsciously mirrored a too-frequent characteristic of the "established," main-line churches: "Bodiform Upholstered Pews: designed for the thousands of members who are demanding more comfort from their churches."

Periodically, such complacency needs to be confronted. Just as Jeremiah carried a word which was like a "hammer that breaks the rock" (23:29) straight into the precincts of the temple, so that word needs to be released today to accomplish the work of disordering and reordering in which lies the church's hope of renewal.

Second Lesson. Commentators on Philippians have speculated that 3:16–19 represents a lengthy interpolation into the original letter. If this is the case, then 3:17–19 and 3:20–4:1 derive from different origins, and the preacher has two texts rather than one on his hands. While it is possible to find a theme that links these two sections of the pericope, there is exegetical justification for preaching from either set of verses without direct reference to the other.

Vv. 17–19 deal with a misunderstanding of Christian freedom which has plagued the church throughout its history. The doctrine of "justification by faith" (at the center of last week's Second Lesson) has been distorted to mean that, since all is of grace, the faithful can be utterly indifferent to works. If God has saved us independent of our works, then the moral quality of a believer's life is a matter of no consequence at all. Thus, the gospel's gift of freedom from the necessity to fulfill the law slips over into unrestrained self-indulgence. This appears to have been the case with those members of the Philippian congregation whom Paul bitterly describes as "enemies of the cross of Christ," whose "god is their belly." They are "enemies of the cross" because they twist the "free grace" of which the cross is the symbol into "cheap grace." Their "god is their belly" because the drive to satisfy their sensual appetites has become idolatrous. (But see the exegesis for an alternate identification of these "enemies.")

The challenge of preaching on this text is that of exposing the current expressions of this same distortion of the gospel without sounding like a middle-aged scold. We live in a culture where instant satisfaction of instant desires has become the norm. Examples range all the way from

prepackaged foods to condensed books to quick drug trips to the possibility of sex without risk to the casual attitude toward abortion. "Satisfaction now!" is our watchword. Restraint and constraint are not popular
in a generation geared to immediate fulfillment, often at the expense of
other persons. A sermon on this text should not only alert Christians to
these contrary pressures in our environment but also set in juxtaposition
to them the peculiar quality of the freedom which is the consequence of
bondage to Christ.

Significantly, Paul provides almost nothing by way of concrete description of this Christian "style of life." He simply calls upon the
Philippians to imitate his example (v. 17). Thomas O'Dea, a sociologist,
has insisted that our most desperate need in this time of spiritual and
moral confusion is for "authentically relevant exemplars" who will in-
carnate the meaning of faith. This suggests an approach to preaching on
the theme here suggested. Rather than talk about characteristics of the
Christian life in general, it will be more potent to hold up portraits of
contemporary saints in action. In this way, people will be provided with
"models" which will begin to shape their own responses to the free gift
of the gospel.

As indicated above, vv. 3:20–4:1 could be dealt with separately, or
they could be related to the theme in vv. 17–19. Paul's image of citizenship in the "commonwealth" of heaven suggests that the Christian is a
colonist, or settler, in this world, participating in the ordinary affairs of
its life, but showing all the characteristics of that homeland to which he
really belongs. The first American colonists who created "little Englands"
up and down the Atlantic seaboard wilderness provide a useful analogy
to the situation of the Christian in society.

Gospel. The parallels between Jesus' confrontation with enemies in
high places and that of Jeremiah has already been noted. The murderous
anger of Herod is part of the gathering storm which will sweep Jesus to
the cross. Yet, he is no passive victim; he deliberately carries the attack
into the heart of enemy territory. He has already "set his face to go to
Jerusalem" (Luke 9:51), and neither warning nor threat will make him
turn back. It's as though he moves forward in the strength of his own
promise to others: "Blessed are those who are persecuted for righteousness' sake, for theirs is the kingdom of heaven" (Matt. 5:9). Preaching on
this text might raise the whole issue of "opposition." Why does the
church live in such relative peace today? Has it lost its capacity to of-

fend? Are its members too securely entrenched in the structures of society to risk challenging those structures? Is the church in danger of becoming just one more respectable institution among many? Of course, martyrdom is not to be courted, but neither is tranquillity to be taken as an unquestionable sign of God's favor. Can the preacher identify points at which absolute faithfulness would lead the "body of Christ" today to contemporary crosses?

The lament which Luke has inserted (see exegesis) beginning with v. 34 has a parallel in the poignant scene of Jesus weeping over Jerusalem (Luke 19:41–44). It has been suggested that two phrases in v. 34 establish the polarities which define the whole relationship between God and man: "Would I . . . you would not." On the one hand, there is God's passionate movement of grace—his powerful yearning for man; on the other hand, there is man's equally passionate opposition to grace—his consistent rejection of God. The paradigm of this polarity is the story of Jesus, the inner meaning of which is summarized in the prologue of the Fourth Gospel: "He was in the world, and the world was made through him, yet the world knew him not. He came to his own home, and his own people received him not" (John 1:10, 11). A sermon could be designed in such a way as to bring to expression this dual mystery of God's unremitting overture and our unrelenting resistance, using this scene of Jesus' approach to Jerusalem and his lament over its self-imposed judgment as a point in history where the mystery is revealed. Further illustration will be found in the ways in which we are constantly offering love and/or refusing to receive love in our relationships with each other.

The Third Sunday in Lent

Lutheran	Roman Catholic	Episcopal	Presbyterian and UCC
Exod. 3:1–8b, 10–15	Exod. 3:1–8a, 13–15	1 Sam. 16:1–13	Exod. 3:1–8, 13–15
1 Cor. 10:1–13	1 Cor. 10:1–6, 10–12	2 Cor. 5:17–21	1 Cor. 10:1–12
Luke 13:1–9	Luke 13:1–9	Luke 13:1–9	Luke 13:1–9

EXEGESIS

First Lesson: Exod. 3:1–8b. A holy place is the setting for the call of Moses, as it later was for Samuel at Shiloh (1 Sam. 3) and Isaiah at

Jerusalem (Isa. 6), and like them Moses receives a prophetic charge, commissioned to speak God's word both to Pharaoh and Israel (cf. Hos. 12:14, which perhaps alludes to our passage). But Moses is also to be something of a military leader like Gideon, who likewise heard the Lord's promise, "I will be with you," when he pleaded unfitness for the task and who also received the promise of a special sign (Judg. 6:16–17). For Moses, however, the "sign" is greatly reduced in order that the story may be given an orientation towards Sinai; Moses is once more a forerunner of the great prophets in that he receives no sign beyond God's continually sustaining him in his task of leadership (Exod. 3:12).

The theophany at the mountain of God has been presented as a prelude to Sinai, but it goes even beyond that to a promise of possessing the "good and spacious land" of Canaan. Such a joining of themes is likely enough the work of later reflection, since the commemoration of God's promise of land seems incongruous at a sanctuary so far from Canaan. God's promise that he himself will lead the people "up" (v. 8) refers to his overall plan, including an allusion to the goal in Canaan; Moses' share is a partial one, for he is to lead the people "out" (vv. 10, 11, 12). God's plan reaches also back to the past, for great emphasis is given to the names of Abraham, Isaac, and Jacob (vv. 6, 15), as if to say that the promises of land which they had received now find their fulfillment in the promise to Moses. Also, patriarchal worship of God under a variety of titles ("God of my father," cf. Exod. 3:6; see also "Kinsman of Isaac," Gen. 31:42, and "Strong One of Jacob," Gen. 49:24) must now yield precedence to the specially revealed name (Exod. 3:15). Since some forms of patriarchal cult may have involved the use of images, the emphasis on Moses' not looking upon the Lord (v. 6; in v. 3 he sees only the flame) may be an attempt to purify the patriarchal heritage.

This desire to link Moses with the earlier period causes a slight inconsistency in the people's supposed question about God's name, for they will have already been told that he is "the God of your fathers" (v. 13). The sacred author accepts this lack of logical sequence in order to synthesize the historical experience of Israel as under the guidance of Yahweh. The revelation of this name itself gives evidence of synthetic effort on the author's part, for he offers three distinct responses of God to Moses' inquiry (vv. 14–15). A whole history is summarized even here. God's first response "I am who I am" originally signified that God is "the Creator," a title closely resembling that used to honor the chief god of the Canaanites ("land flowing with milk and honey" is also drawn from Canaanite poetry). Both this and God's second response "I am" were probably also understood as signifying God's protective presence with Moses ("I am" equals "will be") and with the people. God's existence is thus not encapsuled in a name, but is to be revealed in what he has done and will do (cf. Ezek. 20:38; see also John 10:25, 30).

The mysterious God upon whom man may not gaze and whose very name suggests a fullness that has not yet been totally revealed to man can nonetheless be described with human qualities when his compassion for the people is the issue. He sees, hears, and knows (v. 7), and therefore acts (v. 8), just as Israel was commanded to do (Deut. 4:35–40), but in vain (Deut. 29:3). God does as any compassionate man should, upon seeing a fellow man being led away to his death (Prov. 24:10–12). Such a human image of God expresses the strength of the bond between God and his people, a bond sealed by the revelation of the name that was to be forever proclaimed in liturgical celebration (v. 15).

Second Lesson: 1 Cor. 10:1–13. This warning to the Corinthians is set within a broader context concerning meat sacrificed to idols (8:1–11:1). The sins which Paul opposes here (10:7–10) have their counterparts in the OT, but are also linked to this immediate controversy. He forbids taking part in idolatrous cult itself (10:7, alluding to Exod. 32:6; cf. also 1 Cor. 10:14). His prohibition of lewd conduct (10:8, referring to Num. 25:1–9) is associated with idolatry insofar as the same argument of "freedom" was used by his adversaries to defend both practices (1 Cor. 6:12; 10:23). Paul then warns against testing the Lord (10:9, alluding to Num. 25:5–6), as the Corinthians were doing by sharing in the pagan cultic meals (cf. 10:22). Their grumbling (10:10, combining Exod. 12:23 and Num. 14:36–37) took the form of complaint that even Paul's liberal ruling about food was too restrictive (10:29–30). While forbidding participation in the cult itself, Paul permitted the eating of sacrificial meat in other circumstances, provided no harm was done to the conscience of those less secure in their convictions (10:24–29). Here Paul attempted to steer a middle course between the total freedom advocated by his opponents and the more restrictive attitude represented by the Jerusalem Decree, forbidding any eating of meat sacrificed to idols (Acts 15:29). It is possible that Paul knew of this decree and felt the need to make a special defense of his apostolic authority to adopt his more liberal policy (1 Cor. 9:2, 20–22). This flexibility in the exercise of his ministry was also intended as a model for the Corinthians, as he exhorted them to restraint in the exercise of their freedom (10:32–11:1).

Paul's presentation of the exodus period in our present passage draws much of its inspiration from the book of Wisdom. A large section of this book is devoted to a figurative analysis of Israel's desert experience as symbolic of the future divine judgment and new creation (Wisd. of Sol. 11–19; see especially 17:21; 19:6). This goal of history to some degree colors the presentation of the past events (e.g., the water from the rock signifies God's plan for final judgment, Wisd. of Sol. 11:7–10; the manna as "ambrosial" food symbolizes God's gift of immortality, Wisd. of Sol. 19:21); for Paul also, "the end of the ages" (1 Cor. 10:11) has transformed his description of the past. Here too the food and drink given by God in the desert become symbolic; they are "spiritual," imbued with the power of the Lord who became a "life-giving Spirit" (1 Cor. 15:45). Union with Moses is a being "baptized" (10:2). The rabbinic legend of the traveling rock (v. 4) is probably based on the recurrent appearance of the rock in Exod. 17 and Num. 20 and was formulated to express God's protection for his own in the desert, somewhat like Deut. 8:4; 29:4–5. This legend also is suffused with the NT reality: it "was" Christ.

Such a presentation of history, with its blurring of the distinctions between historical periods and its superimposing of later realities upon earlier, inevitably causes some obscuring of the older events but strikingly illustrates the truth that God's plan rather than the mere sequence of events is the binding force of history. God wills to save, and the reality of that present divine intention was already revealed in Israel's history. In this case, the punishment given to those who partook of God's gifts in the desert reveals that God's present plan of salvation can include punishment for those who think their share in baptism and the Eucharist preserves them from any possible fall, as if they were already safely at the goal (without even need of a resurrection; cf. 1 Cor. 15:12). In calling these OT events "examples" (vv. 6, 11), Paul probably regarded them as more than merely figurative; they already expressed to some degree the same divine work of salvation revealed in Christ. Their quality of "example" partakes of his own "imitation" of Christ (11:1), as Paul's frequent linking of "example" and "imitation" indicates (1 Thess. 1:6–7; 2 Thess. 3:9; Phil. 3:17; for the Pauline sense of "imitation," cf. the commentary on Phil. 3:17–4:1 from last Sunday).

Gospel: Luke 13:1–9. This reading preserves a tension in Jesus' own understanding of his mission. He preached the urgent need to decide in favor of personal reform because judgment was imminent (vv. 1–5) and yet regarded his own ministry as a postponement of the judgment, a sign of God's mercy allowing further time for repentance (vv. 6–9). The prior section (vv. 1–5) contains two warnings identically structured: rhetorical question, negative response, and appeal for reform. It is possible that the examples themselves are related. The first, Pilate's massacre of the Galileans, is undoubtedly based on real or suspected revolutionary activity on the part of these pilgrims to Jerusalem; the Galilean origin of Jesus would later be brought before Pilate in order to raise a similar suspicion against him (Luke 23:5). The second, the collapse of the Siloam tower, may have also involved zealot opposition to Pilate; the Jewish historian Josephus informs us that Jews opposed Pilate's appropriation of temple funds for the construction of an aqueduct. Perhaps the enmity broke out into open conflict near the pool of Siloam. In this second example, only conjecture is possible, since neither episode in vv. 1–5 is known from any other source. However, some association with violent revolt against Roman authority makes it easier to see why such episodes could give rise to discussion about God's justice and man's sinfulness, particularly in the prior case where the offering of sacrifice would more likely, of itself, suggest martyrdom rather than sinfulness. But whatever the background of these episodes, it is striking that Jesus refuses to judge either innocence or guilt but turns them into occasions for personal scrutiny and decision.

The notification of Jesus about Pilate's action (v. 1) should be understood as a warning given to Jesus, who was also a Galilean on his way to Jerusalem (13:22); it parallels the warning about Herod in this same chapter (v. 31). We have a foreboding of the future association of these two rulers in the death of Jesus. In 13:1 we find a basis for the rift between them, since the Galileans were under Herod's jurisdiction rather than Pilate's; this enmity will be healed when they later defer to each other in sending Jesus back and forth between them (23:6–12). On this occasion, Luke detracts from the guilt of Pilate in Jesus' death (23:14, 15, 20, 22), while making it clear that Pilate retained ultimate responsibility (23:24, 25, 52). However, in chap. 13, he underlines the heinousness of what Pilate has done. His puzzling description of Pilate's action as "mixing" the blood of the Galileans with their sacrifices, while its precise meaning is not clear, at least depicts the slaughter as performed during the sacrifice itself and thus approximates their fate to that of Zechariah, who died between the altar and the sanctuary (11:51), during the liturgy itself (cf. Joel 2:17).

The parable of the fig tree recalls several OT passages, such as the care expended on the vineyard in Isa. 5:1–2. Here the emphasis is on a fig tree rather than the vineyard itself, perhaps because Luke wishes to modify Jesus' cursing of the fig tree (Mark 11:12–14). The three barren years followed by a year for reform recalls the regulation concerning fruit trees in Lev. 19:23–25: for three years the fruit of a newly planted tree is not to be eaten, while that of the fourth year is to be left totally for the Lord. Such a theme fits well with Luke's theology, which characterizes the public ministry of Jesus as a "year of favor" (Luke 4:19).

This parable, with its OT allusions, its share in the Lucan theology of Christ's ministry, and its lack of a concluding response by the owner of the vineyard, probably owes much to Lucan formulation, but also appears close to Jesus' interpretation of his own ministry. It is also of service to Luke in dealing with the situation of the church of his own day. It was necessary to keep alive the expectation of Christ's return (Luke 18:7–8) and yet allow for a whole new age, the growth of the church under the guidance of the Holy Spirit (cf. Acts, in general). Luke's understanding of Christ's mission probably allowed him to look upon the period of the church as a prolonging of the opportunity for salvation (cf. 2 Pet. 3:9, 15). But for the period of the church, the emphasis remains more on the urgency of reform rather than the period of reprieve. God's withholding of punishment characterizes more the ages past rather than the age of the church (Acts 17:30–31). It is preeminently the words of Jesus about reform that Luke directs to the Christians of his own day (Luke 13:3, 5; cf. also 13:28–29, where Luke clearly applies to Christians a saying originally directed against a Jewish audience, Matt. 8:11–12).

HOMILETICAL INTERPRETATION

The lessons for Oculi, the Third Sunday in Lent, fit into a more consistent pattern than is the case with most of the other Sundays of this season. This means that it will be possible to preach on any one of these texts, while, in connection with it, making major reference to one of the others. In particular, two themes begin to emerge as one reflects upon these three lessons:

1. The problem of suffering. This is raised by Jesus, in the first half of the Gospel, in the form of this question: "Is suffering the result of sin?" Jesus denies the possibility of finding such a cause-and-effect chain in every instance of human suffering. The Second Lesson, on the other hand, suggests that *some* suffering may be a sign of judgment. The First Lesson does not address the issue of causality. It rather presents a moving picture of the God who, whatever the reason for suffering, identifies himself with those who are its victims. This is a revelation which reaches its climax in the cross which stands at the end of our Lenten journey.

2. The question of judgment. This is not unrelated to the problem of suffering, but the Second Lesson focuses it in a particular way. It asks, in effect, "Are those who are sacramentally part of the church thereby automatically insured against all judgment?" Paul's clear answer is "No!" Jesus' brief parable of the vinedresser points in the same direction, especially when it is remembered that the vine was a symbol for Israel and later for the church.

The introit, with its plea, "Turn unto me, and have mercy upon me: for I am desolate and afflicted," and the collect, with its petition that God shall "stretch forth the right hand of [his] Majesty to be our defense against all our enemies," are both clearly appropriate to the themes articulated in the lections.

First Lesson. This reading is one of the great "call" passages of the Bible. The preacher will feel the attractiveness of making Moses the center of attention in his sermon. Moses can be seen as an outstanding exemplar of the life of faith: he hears God's call, he is initially overwhelmed and reluctant to surrender to it, but finally he entrusts himself to the God who both summons him and promises to support him.

Alternatively, it is possible to focus on Moses not so much in terms of the biographical elements in this passage but in terms of his being a "type" of Christ. Jesus was sometimes designated by the earliest church as a "second Moses," or the "one greater than Moses." This was possible because the first Christians viewed Jesus, like Moses, as a "deliverer" whom God, seeing the desolations of his people, had sent to rescue them from their bondage. In his own Nazareth sermon, Jesus had identified himself with that servant through whom God had promised "to proclaim release to the captives" (Luke 4:18*b*). "Deliverance from bondage," whether personal or social, is a way of looking at the work of the gospel and the mission of the church, and can provide a proper preaching theme from this text.

While the approaches suggested above have their legitimacy, there is a sense in which to focus on Moses is to place the wrong figure at center stage. This passage is not so much revelatory of Moses as of God. Above all, it discloses a God of compassion, i.e., one who literally "suffers with" his people. The clue is in v. 7: "I have seen the affliction of my people who are in Egypt, and have heard their cry because of their taskmasters; I know their sufferings." Here, already in the history of Israel, as later in the death on Golgotha, there is revealed to us the God who refuses to stand aloof from human pain but participates in it.

There is scarcely any preaching theme more urgently in need of development today. For all the vaunted affluence and technological advance in our society, there is a throbbing agony just below the surface. Certain place names have become symbols of it—Dachau, Buchenwald, Hiroshima, Watts, Detroit, Vietnam. Our generation may have been exposed to more mass agony (not to mention each man's private agony) than any in history, and, as Bonhoeffer remind us, in such a world "only a suffering God will do." A God untouched by the pain of his creation and his creatures is simply unbelievable. But in the cross we have the sign, torn out of God's own heart, that he is "the great Companion, the fellow-sufferer who understands" (A. N. Whitehead). Here, indeed, is good news which every congregation—whether it be filled with the disinherited ("in Egypt") or with the affluent (in the "land flowing with milk and honey")—needs to hear.

Second Lesson. This lesson, replete with OT allusions, is illustrative of Paul's own way of interpreting the OT "christologically." The ancient Scripture was not only a book for the Jews; it was a book for the church, "written down for our instruction" (v. 11), in the age when all foreshadowed there was being fulfilled. All that had happened to "old Israel" was a sign of God's dealings with "new Israel." We may not be able to adopt Paul's intricate and detailed allegorizing (vv. 1–6) as a hermeneutical principle; nevertheless, his underlying conviction that there is a unity between God's address to Israel through the events of her history and his address to us through the event of Jesus is still sound.

At the center of Paul's concern in this passage is a false "sacramentalism," whether in Israel or the church. Already he had spotted within the Christian community persons who were presuming on their participation in the cultic life of the "body" as the warranty of their salvation. The allusions to baptism and the Lord's Supper in vv. 4 through 6 suggest that there were Christians who were saying, "Because God has put his seal on me in my baptism and because I regularly renew my covenant at the table, I'm immune from all judgment. I'm automatically 'in'." It is significant that Paul—that indefatigable preacher of unconditional grace—declares, "No!" It's not that new "conditions" are now attached to God's absolutely free offer. It's only that Christians can't presume on that gift. They aren't free to live as though it had never been given. In fact, to persist unchanged in the patterns of the old life is to expose the terrible reality that, in spite of sacramental signs, no gift has been received. It's like overprivileged children who, surrounded by the best educational and cultural advantages available, still betray no signs of such exposure in their character.

The preacher must take great care in developing this theme not to compromise the central NT affirmation that justification is by *grace*, not works; yet, at the same time, he must help disabuse his people of any automatism with respect to sacramental grace. Paul's words about exercising self-control and pummeling his own body, in the verses immediately preceding this lection, are a healthy corrective of any view that sharply separates justification from sanctification, or freedom from discipline (cf. 1 Cor. 15:10). A key word in this whole passage is the powerful "nevertheless" at the beginning of v. 5. God speaks a great "nevertheless" to us when, in spite of our unrighteousness, he declares us righteous. Here he declares another "nevertheless" which functions when, in spite of his unutterable generosity, we live as though nothing had changed. The dual usages of this single word can provide a unifying theme for a sermon.

The catalogue of things with which "God was not pleased" in vv. 6 through 10 are references to events in the wilderness wanderings of Israel. Paul sees parallels in the situation he confronts in the congregation in Corinth. It will be the modern preacher's task to find convincing examples of the concrete forms which such sins as idolatry, immorality, testing God, and grumbling take in his situation.

Nor should the preacher overlook the fact that this lesson ends on a note of promise rather than of doom. It will be easy to produce from a passage so full of warning a sermon which does no more than beat the faithful black and blue. Christians, beleagured on every side by pressures to relax their discipleship, need to know that God struggles with us against every force which threatens to separate us from himself. "He's by our side upon the plain with His good gifts and Spirit" (Luther). This is a truth which has already been opened up for us in the Gospel for the First Sunday in Lent.

Gospel. The note of judgment heard in the Second Lesson echoes also in the Gospel for this Sunday. The proper context for the appointed passage from Luke reaches back into vv. 54 through 59 of the preceding chapter. Here Jesus chides the crowds for being good-weather prophets while remaining almost illiterate when it comes to reading the "signs of the time." They fail to see the crisis of judgment his coming has precipitated. In rejecting his offer of and demand for love, Israel is accelerating its headlong plunge into catastrophe. Are there such signs on the moral and spiritual horizon today? Where is our society rushing precipitously toward the brink? Prophets like Martin Luther King were sounding warnings for us in the 60s. We ignored them at great cost. The explosions in our cities were in large measure the direct consequences of our neglect of the poor and our oppression of blacks. There's a sense in which preaching is an exercise in such prognostication—raising storm warnings for an unwary community or nation before it's too late.

The message of judgment takes a peculiar twist in the verses appointed for the Gospel. Jesus cites two public calamities, the kind of events which would have had nationwide television coverage today. Some were saying that God had singled out these particular victims because they were especially grievous sinners. According to the old Jewish formula, righteousness leads to prosperity and sin to adversity. Therefore, these disasters must have been God's way of punishing those whose offenses were more heinous than others. Jesus objected to such a simplistic causality. He would have agreed with the author of the book of Job in his argument that it's impossible to draw precise connections between specific sins and specific instances of suffering. Nevertheless, vv. 3 and 5 indicate that Jesus saw *some* connection between collective sin and collective suffering. When whole peoples order their corporate life by injustice or violence, they must be prepared for tragic consequences. Those who sow to the wind will invariably reap the whirlwind.

The problem Jesus addresses here is by no means obsolete. Every pastor has heard the anguished question, "What did I do to deserve this?" Behind that question lurks a theology which sees God as an angry father, meting out some punishment for every disobedience of his children. Of course, if this were God's way with us, we would all be subject to more pain than we are. But such a theology has not even caught up with the faith of the author of Ps. 103:10 ("He hath not dealt with us after our sins: nor rewarded us according to our iniquities"), let alone a view of God which roots in the cross. This text affords an opportunity to address this misunderstanding head on, and, coupled with the First Lesson, to lead people to a deeper understanding of God's relationship to human suffering.

The preacher should also note that, while the brief parable in vv. 6 through 9 continues the theme of judgment, its central message is of God's patience. He struggles with his people against every condition contrary to their "fruitfulness." The word is: "Don't presume on God's patience; but never despair of it."

The Fourth Sunday in Lent

Lutheran	*Roman Catholic*	*Episcopal*	*Presbyterian and UCC*
Isa. 12:1–6	Josh. 5:9a–12	Isa. 12	Josh. 5:9–12
1 Cor. 1:18–31	2 Cor. 5:17–21	Eph. 2:4–10	2 Cor. 5:16–21
Luke 15:1–3, 11–32	Luke 15:1–3, 11–32	Luke 15:11–32	Luke 15:11–32

EXEGESIS

First Lesson: Isa. 12:1–6. The praise offered to God in this passage is a response to the future saving action of God, described in the preceding section as a new exodus (11:10–16, especially vv. 15–16). The author is not Isaiah himself, for whom the exodus was not a major theme. He is probably writing after the Babylonian exile, since he adopts the viewpoint of one who is already settled in the holy land (11:14) and who has already experienced the rivalries of the postexilic period (11:13; cf. Neh. 3:33–38).

The first brief hymn (12:1–2) is reminiscent of several psalms of thanksgiving proclaimed by an unnamed individual (cf. Pss. 9, 30, and

138; note "I will give you thanks" in Ps. 30:13). In these three psalms, the individual may have been the king speaking in the name of the people (cf. Ps. 9:16; 30:8; 138:4). Even though a royal figure is also prominent in our context (Isa. 11:1–5, 10), it is likely that the one addressed by the prophet in Isa. 12:1 is actually the people itself, regarded as an individual, much as the city of Jerusalem is addressed as a single person in 12:6. The prophet speaks to one who is apparently a contemporary (12:1); since there was no king in his day, he probably addressed the community. A form of praise originally spoken by an individual has now become the prayer of the people (cf. Ps. 69, especially vv. 36–37).

This first prayer also draws upon other sources, notably the ancient song of Moses (Exod. 15:1–18; cf. Isa. 12:2; Exod. 15:2), thus reinforcing the theme of a new exodus. The combination of "salvation" and "comfort" recalls various passages in Second Isaiah (Isa. 40–55, written during the Babylonian exile), particularly 49:6–13; 51:3–13; and 52:7–10. Sprinkled throughout these three passages are other themes which have shaped Isa. 12:1–6, such as exodus, Jerusalem, God's gift of water, the "Holy One," and the worldwide proclamation of God's deeds.

The second brief hymn (vv. 3–6) is introduced by the first part of v. 3; this introduction preserves the spirit of the first hymn, for it recalls both the exodus (cf. Ps. 114:8) and Second Isaiah (Isa. 41:18–20), even while retaining its own unique formulation ("fountain of salvation"). The community is now addressed in the plural form (v. 4), for they appear as a group, exhorting one another to praise. The language of v. 4 is drawn from Pss. 105:1–5 and 148:13, hymns of praise where no particular individual emerges, whereas in v. 5 the author composes in more original fashion. He has thus creatively reshaped traditional language and applied it to what is to come. Here he differs from the former usage of thanksgiving psalms, which proclaimed gratitude for what God had already accomplished. Ps. 118 is close in tenor to our passage (it also cites Exod. 15:2, as Isa. 12:2 does; cf. Ps. 118:14), but the "today" of Ps. 118:14 here becomes "that day" of the future. And yet the author's personal expression of praise cannot remain entirely future, since it springs from his present faith and will continually nourish the faith of his readers. He approaches the gratitude of Jesus in John 11:41, who thanks his Father even before the Father responds.

Our passage draws upon ancient liturgical texts, but is itself not joined to any feast. It is the prayer of any Israelite in any situation on that future "day." Though addressed to a community, it is a product of the author's personal trust, akin to the prayers prompted by the reflections of Ben Sirach (cf. Ecclus. 23:1-6; 36:1-17). Its spirit is reflected in the spontaneous praise offered by Jesus when he exclaimed, "I praise you, O Father" (Luke 10:21; Matt. 11:25). Here Jesus draws upon the ancient prayers of thanksgiving. As in Ps. 138, the lowly and the proud are part of God's plan (Luke 10:21; Ps. 138:6); as in that same psalm and our present passage, the personal expression of praise leads into a revelation granted to others (Ps. 138:4; Isa. 12:4-5; Luke 10:22).

Second Lesson: 1 Cor. 1:18-31. It was traditional that wisdom be discussed insofar as it contrasts with foolishness (e.g., Prov. 12; Wisd. of Sol. 2). Our present context in Paul treats this dichotomy at length (1 Cor. 1-4); in fact, except for one brief mention (Rom. 1:22), it is only in these chapters that Paul ever discusses the theme of "foolishness." We may surmise that his opponents also made use of the wise-foolish antinomy in order to disparage Paul's teaching. Paul accepts the charge and affirms that his teaching is indeed absurdity. The conflict centers around Paul's understanding of the cross. For a Jew, the mere past historical event of crucifixion would be a stumbling block to belief (1 Cor. 1:23), especially because of Deut. 21:23. But for Paul, the foolishness goes even beyond the crucifixion as past event, for he elsewhere notes that the cross would not be an obstacle if he were also willing to preach the need of circumcision (Gal. 5:11). Rather, Paul insists that the cross of Jesus must be understood as it relates to the present. Jesus is not preached except as crucified (1 Cor. 2:2), and his cross must not be robbed of its present meaning (1:17). To the Corinthians, conscious of the richness of their gifts (1:5-6), to find present meaning in the death of Christ must have seemed foolish; with Christ they had now already reached perfection (4:8). But Paul affirms that the cross expressed a pattern of life to be experienced now; his reference to the humble origins of the Corinthian community (1:26-31) aptly illustrates how the lowliness of the cross is still present among them.

Mere human understanding cannot grasp such a teaching. Paul's own experience at Athens shortly before he founded the Corinthian church probably helped to convince him of this truth. The book of Wisdom spoke of men's foolishness leading them to idolatry (Wisd. of Sol. 12:24) and at Athens Paul found it was so (Acts 17:16; cf. Rom. 1:22-23). Both there and at Corinth, Paul's hearers balked at the concept "raising of the dead" (cf. Acts 17:32 and 1 Cor. 15:12). Despite differences between the two occasions, both groups probably shared a reluctance to extend God's saving work to the human body. Paul's opponents at Corinth could then logically conclude that bodily life or death had no real meaning; all that counted was the gifts of the Spirit which they already possessed.

In order further to counter such supposed wisdom, Paul draws upon prophets who combated the "wise men" (royal advisers) of their own day. He is indebted to Isaiah in 1 Cor. 1:19–20 (cf. Isa. 29:14; 19:12; 33:18); the words of both men rebuke the wise men of their respective times for an overhasty affirmation of salvation without reference to the gradual working out of God's plan (cf. Isa. 5:19). The words of Jeremiah, on the other hand, are prominent in the concluding verses concerning the humble origins of the community (vv. 26–31). The classes of people considered (v. 26) are a variation upon Jer. 9:22; the concluding verse (1 Cor. 1:31) modifies Jer. 9:23; this latter verse of Jeremiah has probably also contributed to 1 Cor. 1:30. To the "justice" of Jer. 9:23, Paul could readily add "sanctification" as a description of man's present state in faith (cf. 1 Cor. 6:11 and Rom. 6:19); the further addition of "redemption" shifts the perspective towards man's future goal (Rom. 8:23).

This entire discussion of wisdom is set within the context of Paul's response to the fragmentation of the community (1 Cor. 1:10). Even though baptism expressed so richly Paul's theology of Christian life as partaking in Christ's cross (1 Cor. 6:3–5; cf. also 1 Cor. 1:13), the rite itself needs the "word" of interpretation (1:18). Without such an understanding, new converts apparently looked on the rite as giving them a special link to an illustrious personage in the church (1:12–13). They were carried away like Simon Magus when he was baptized and became "a disciple of Philip" (Acts 8:13), himself a man of power and wisdom (Acts 6:3; 8:6). Against any such partisanship, Paul recalls the faithful to the unity they have in Christ alone (1 Cor. 2:2).

Gospel: Luke 15:1–3, 11–32. Our parable builds upon a system of legal relationships in order to depict a love which goes beyond the provisions of law. The father of the two sons agrees to transfer to them ownership of his property (v. 12); after the younger son departs with his share, the elder is the sole owner (v. 31), but the father retains the right to administer the property during his own lifetime (vv. 29–30). The younger son's sin against his father is probably his destruction of the father's possibility of ever drawing any benefit from the younger son's share, unless we are simply to think that his dissolute living is a disgrace to his parents (Prov. 17:21, 25). The parable moves to another level in order to express the gratuitous love of a father-son relationship. This reaches its high point in the father's joy, expressed in the banquet for his newly returned son (v. 24). The elder son, on the other hand, does not grasp the meaning of sonship; he refers to his own life as that of a slave (v. 29) and refrains from using the respectful title "father" (v. 29). Consequently, he cannot accept the younger son as his brother (v. 30).

The father in this parable should not be identified with God the Father, not merely because his dividing of the property may show a lack of wisdom (cf. Ecclus. 33:18–24), but also because both the father and God appear as distinct persons in the parable (vv. 18, 21). Nonetheless, the human father expresses the joy attributed to God himself in 15:7, 10 (Semitic idiom here avoids direct mention of God's name), and recalls the love of God offering his "son" Israel a new home (Hos. 11). This human father also is a sign of what Jesus is doing as he welcomes sinners with festive joy (Luke 5:33–34). This binding of the joy of God and that of Jesus into the single image of a father's love suggests John 14:9, "Whoever has seen me has seen the Father."

This joy arises from the final victory over Satan as a reality already to some degree experienced in the ministry of Jesus (Luke 10:17–18). This sense of ultimate triumph is expressed in our parable through the theme of "life from death." The younger son was "perishing" (v. 17), but then "rose up" (v. 18); his father rejoices to have him back again in good "health" (compare Luke 5:31 and 15:27) and twice affirms that the boy returned from death (vv. 24, 32). This descent into death and the return to life is a theme also expressed in the movement from sonship to servitude (v. 15) and even symbolically to the level of the pigs themselves (v. 16), animals whose ritual uncleanness left the young man in a living "death"; the direction reverses as he returns to receive the ring and robe as signs of authority in the family (cf. Gen. 41:42; 1 Macc. 6:15). The father does not allow him to voice his request to become a servant (cf. vv. 21–22); rather, one of the servants will bring the young man shoes as a sign of his superiority (cf. Luke 3:16; Isa. 20:2; cf. also Gal. 4:6–7).

The central moment in this return from death is repentance. Luke has already given emphasis to this theme in the closely related passage concerning the conversion of Levi (5:27–32; this last verse mentions "repentance," merely implicit in Mark 2:17 and Matt. 9:13); repentance is expressly mentioned as the reason for joy in heaven (15:7, 10), even though the examples employed do not directly concern the theme of conversion (15:4–5, 8–9); in the present parable it is given special place through a description of the process of inner conversion (15:17–20).

The new life offered in the ministry of Jesus is expressed by Luke in his noting that Jesus "welcomed" sinners (Luke 15:1). God's gift of sonship is made present in the meals Jesus shared with sinners. For Jesus, any believer was a member of his "family" (Luke 8:21). It is not likely that the Pharisees and scribes (15:2) correspond exactly to the older brother, but the persuasive words of the father are indirectly an invitation to them to see God's mercy at work in what Jesus is doing.

HOMILETICAL INTERPRETATION

"Laetare!" "Rejoice!" This opening imperative of the introit for today provides the traditional title for the Fourth Sunday in Lent. A note of joy suddenly rings out in the midst of the more somber music of judgment we have been hearing. "Rejoice ye with Jerusalem, and be glad with her: all ye that love her. Rejoice for joy with her: all ye that mourn for her." The mood is all the more striking, because next Sunday—especially in the Gospel—the theme of judgment will return fortissimo.

Today, however, all the appointed lections echo the jubilant theme announced in the introit. The First Lesson from Isaiah is actually a song of praise: "With joy you will draw water from the wells of salvation. . . . Shout, and sing for joy, O inhabitant of Zion." The Second Lesson, while not explicitly mentioning joy, contains Paul's tribute to the cross in which is revealed "God's foolishness which is wiser than men," and his weakness which "is stronger than men." The Gospel—the parable of the prodigal son—climaxes in a boisterous homecoming feast in which a father "makes merry" because a son who was dead "is alive again."

It is to be noted, though, that there is nothing superficial or lighthearted about the joy which resounds through these lessons. It has nothing in common with any Mardi Gras mood of "eat, drink, and be merry." This is a joy which has been wrung out of tragedy; it lies on the other side of anguish. It is neither the innocent joy of childhood nor the reckless abandon of the playboy. Jesus expressed its quality precisely when he said: "When a woman is in travail she has sorrow, because her hour has come; but when she is delivered of the child, she no longer remembers the anguish, for joy that a child is born into the world. So you have sorrow now, but I will see you again and your hearts will rejoice, and no one will take your joy from you" (John 16:21, 22). Thus, as we noted on Ash Wednesday, Lent is not a season of unrelieved penitence. While we contemplate the sin in us and in our world which made necessary the cross, we also know that in the cross lies the secret of life and hope—"the power of God and the wisdom of God," as Paul puts it. Therefore, we rejoice and give thanks for this invincible grace which can turn death into life. But it is a sober joy and a chastened celebration, because we cannot fail to remember that "he was bruised for our iniquities . . . and with his stripes we are healed" (Isa. 53:5).

First Lesson. As the exegesis indicates, we are dealing here with a psalmlike song of praise which has been inserted into the text of Isaiah. The historical context is uncertain, but the phrase "in that day" suggests a time of hardship from which a confidently-hoped-for deliverance lies still in the future. This fits nicely the liturgical setting in which the church hears this lesson: we are passing through the time of penitence, with the deliverance wrought on Good Friday and Easter still lying ahead of us. But we move on with joyous expectation, for we know that "God is faithful."

The problem of preaching on any poetic passage lies in its profusion of images. It is difficult to encompass them all in one sermon, so it is often best to center in on only one of those offered. With this "psalm," however, there is a good opportunity to let the sweep of the whole composition determine the structure of the sermon. In its entirety it is a song in praise of God's triumphant grace. It will be necessary for the preacher —probably early in the sermon—to speak realistically about the plight from which we need deliverance. Such terms as guilt, anxiety, meaninglessness, confusion, come to mind. Then the progress of the verses themselves almost provides an outline to speak about the grace—decisively operative in Jesus' death and resurrection and available to us through his body, the church—which reaches us in the midst of our need: (1) the fact of grace (vv. 1, 2); (2) the sources of grace (v. 3); (3) the celebration of grace (vv. 5a, 6); (4) the witness to grace (vv. 46, 56).

Should the preacher choose to focus on a single image, v. 3 is immediately attractive: "With joy you will draw water from the wells of salvation." In semiarid Palestine, a dependable well has always seemed a gift not to be taken for granted. Drought for crops and thirst for animals and men were ever-present threats. It is no wonder, therefore, that water took on symbolic, even eschatological meaning in Hebrew thought. The author of the Fourth Gospel is following in this same tradition when he has Jesus say of himself: "Whoever drinks of the water that I shall give him will never thirst; the water that I shall give him will become in him a spring of water welling up to eternal life" (John 4:14).

It will not be difficult to describe the aridity of contemporary life. In our feverish, plastic, thing-centered age, people often find little to satisfy their profound thirst for renewal of faith, hope, and love. T. S. Eliot's lines are descriptive of our condition:

> Here is no water but only rock
> Rock and no water and the sandy road
> The road winding above among the mountains
> Which are mountains of rock without water.[1]

The church, with its gospel, its sacraments, and its community of love, invites those who thirst to come to inexhaustible "wells" from which they can draw living water with joy.

Second Lesson. Paul sets the gospel in sharp contrast to elements which characterized the culture in which he preached. For Jews, on the lookout for some spectacular demonstration that the messianic kingdom had arrived with power, the message of a crucified One seemed abject weakness. For Greeks, demanding some logically compelling and rationally satisfying structure of thought, the blunt announcement that ultimate truth was to be found in an executed Jewish peasant seemed utter nonsense. The cross could hardly have been designed to be more offensive to the most religiously (the Jews) and intellectually (the Greeks) "advanced" people of Paul's time.

The task of the preacher today is to identify those elements in our culture to which the gospel is such a stark offense. It may be that "wisdom" and "power" are still the most likely candidates. Certainly our era is obsessed with both. We admire "wisdom," whether in the shrewd operator or in the brilliant researcher and planner. Education, at the highest level possible for every citizen, is a national goal. We expect our

1. T. S. Eliot, *The Wasteland and Other Poems* (New York: Harcourt, Brace and Co., 1934), p. 42.

most complex problems, personal or social, to yield to hard thought; and, surely, the contributions of the life of the mind to our society are not to be minimized. Likewise, "power" is very close to the center of our concern—all the way from "flower power" to nuclear power. How to persuade, impress, coerce, or prevail exercises us daily, whether in business, politics, or family life; and, surely, power in its various forms is necessary for the functioning of life.

Yet, the gospel stands in radical opposition to our customary definitions of "wisdom" and "power." God has his own way of turning upside down all our human expectations with regard to them:

> They all were looking for a king
> To slay their foes and lift them high:
> Thou cam'st, a little baby thing
> That made a woman cry.[2]

Even more dramatically than the nativity, the cross, to which all roads lead during Lent, reveals the strange shape of God's kind of "wisdom" and "power." He offers neither an unmistakable exhibition of power nor an impressive system of thought but only a small-town carpenter bleeding on a cross. No hint of power; only abject helplessness—yet the potency of that act of suffering love will never be spent. No beautifully rational idea; only the horror of blood and pain—yet a source of truth and life beyond all understanding. And this mystery of God's strange "wisdom" and "power" continues in his choice of those whom the world would be inclined to reject to create his church. As someone has said, "God is a potter; he works in mud."

Gospel. Taking their cue from the setting Luke provides for the three parables of "the lost" in this chapter, exegetes today generally see the target of the parable of the prodigal son to be not wayward sinners in need of forgiveness but self-righteous "saints" who begrudge God's mercy to others. The parable thus becomes a means by which Jesus justifies to his opponents his own mission among the outcasts in Israel. If they criticize him for his table-fellowship with prostitutes and publicans, then they must know that in the same breath they are criticizing God. Jesus' own welcome of those who can no longer hide their desperate need is a

2. George MacDonald, "That Holy Thing," in *The World's Great Religious Poetry* (New York: Macmillan, 1943), p. 327.

reflex of God's mercy for the sinner, of which the father's joyous embrace of his returned son in the parable is a dramatic representation. Approached from this angle, the parable can lead to a sermon on the mission of the church. It raises uncomfortable questions for the faithful who, like the older brother (and the Pharisees of Jesus' time), are dutifully meeting their religious and moral "obligations." Does such formal "righteousness" too easily slip over into "self-righteousness"? Do rectitude and responsibility tend to narrow our view of who belongs in the household of faith? Why does moral uprightness so often combine with emotional "uptightness"—paralyzing the outward flow of compassion? The consequence is to be seen in congregations whose range for evangelism is no broader than the "OK world" of us and ours.

Though the parable, in its original purpose, has this edge of judgment, its point is made by a moving portrayal of the openness of God to all who turn to him. The word "prodigal," traditionally associated with the parable but nowhere mentioned in it, can provide a key for another homiletical approach to it. "Prodigal" means literally "extravagant," "wasteful," "spendthrift." With that definition in mind, it is possible to read the parable as the story of not one prodigal but three. First, and most obviously, there is the younger son, running through his inheritance as though it were water and finding himself in the desolation which always follows the misuse of freedom. Second, there is the older brother, performing his tasks on the farm dutifully (but, one suspects, lovelessly), and squandering months or years of opportunity to discover the true meaning of home and sonship. He was as far from his father as was his younger brother in the distant city. Finally, there is the father himself. What could be more extravagant than the welcome he gives to his wastrel son, or even the gentle response to the angry outburst of the older brother? To both, he gladly turns his heart inside out, nothing held back, nothing asked by way of surety or condition. Robert Frost has pinpointed the message of the story in a line from one of his poems: home is "something you somehow haven't to deserve."[3] The preacher can find imaginative ways of bringing each of these "prodigals" alive in modern dress. And he will point somewhere to the One whose life, death, and resurrection make believable the reality of grace reflected in this matchless story.

3. Robert Frost, *Robert Frost's Poems* (New York: Pocket Books, Inc., 1956), p. 166.

The Fifth Sunday in Lent

Lutheran	Roman Catholic	Episcopal	Presbyterian and UCC
Isa. 43:16–21	Isa. 43:16–21	Isa. 43:16–21	Isa. 43:16–21
Phil. 3:8–14	Phil. 3:8–14	Phil. 2:12–15	Phil. 3:8–14
Luke 20:9–19	John 8:1–11	Mark 12:1–11	Luke 22:14–30

EXEGESIS

First Lesson: Isa. 43:16–21. Speaking in the name of God, an anonymous prophet, author of Isa. 40–55, addresses Israelites living in Babylonia during the period of the exile. He has become enthused at victories the Persians have already won (43:3) and rouses the people to share his vision of a forthcoming return to the promised land. God's saving action is already "budding forth" (v. 19), an expression which reawakens hopes attached to the future Davidic king, the "Righteous Shoot" (Jer. 23:5). This prophet, known as Second Isaiah, gives little emphasis to the king himself, but the blessings linked with the monarchy in the past are still the object of hope (Isa. 55:3). For Second Isaiah, the Persian Cyrus would be a source of blessing by overcoming Babylon; as a "shepherd" of the Lord (Isa. 44:28), Cyrus would show kindness to the Israelites, allowing them to return home (2 Chron. 36:22–23). Like the Egyptians, Babylon would be snuffed out like a wick (Isa. 43:17), but the smoking wick of Israel would not be quenched (42:3).

This view toward the future shapes our entire passage. The older simple expression, "Thus says the Lord" (v. 16), is embellished with a series of phrases recalling the events of the exodus (vv. 16–17); these actions are here no longer past, but become timeless attributes of God. Thus they prepare the way for the divine message itself: "Remember not the events of the past" (v. 18). Such language as this fits well with Second Isaiah's frequent use of creation themes to speak of God's action for his people. Creation is not merely a past event, for God still sustains all things (e.g., Isa. 40:26, 28); likewise, his past actions of salvation describe his present and future deeds. His saving acts are actually a form of "creation." His "forming" of the people (43:21) recalls the act of "forming" man from clay (cf. 43:7; 45:9; see also Gen. 2:7). The "mighty waters" opened up by the Lord (Isa. 43:16) are a distant echo of the myth which pictured the sea as a hostile force vanquished by God at creation (cf. Job 26:13; Isa. 51:9; see also Exod. 14:16), a theme found analogously in the liturgy of the surrounding Babylonians. God's dominion over all creation inspires the prophet to speak of him as "leading out" the Egyptians (Isa. 43:17), an expression usually employed to describe rather his relationship to his own people (Exod. 6:7; Deut. 13:6). Since God's saving action is a form of creation, no limit is placed on the newness of future possibilities. The jackal and ostrich were signs of desolation and destruction (cf. Isa. 13:21–22), but now their mournful sounds (Mic. 1:8) become a "giving glory" (Isa. 43:20); thus these animals join the people in "giving glory" to God in sounds of praise. Formerly, God made a path through water (v. 16), but now, paradoxically, water will mark out the path through dry land (v. 19). Here Second Isaiah built upon authentic words of Jeremiah about the restoration of the northern kingdom (Jer. 31:9); disciples of Jeremiah apparently reversed the process later as they structured Jer. 23:5–8 as a parallel to our passage (vv. 18–19). Perhaps this theme of water took on extra richness for Second Isaiah because his contemporaries viewed it as a symbol for God's revelation and built into several passages in Exodus a close association between God's word and his gift of water (cf. Exod. 15:25; 17:6). For Second Isaiah, to receive the blessings of God's word was a drinking of water (Isa. 55:1; see also John 7:37–38); the word itself came down like rain or snow (Isa. 55:10–11).

This reading looks forward to a new "remembrance" (v. 18), thus a liturgy of the future. Much of Second Isaiah's language resembles a hymn and suggests that his own words anticipate the worship which is to come. The repeated exhortations throughout his writing indirectly show that he probably won little support for his efforts, even though his words were "good news" (cf. Isa. 52:7). Thus he also anticipates the efforts of Jesus, whose message of God's love was too much for many to accept (cf. Luke 13:34).

Second Lesson: Phil. 3:8–14. This portion of the epistle expresses Paul's attempt to assess the meaning of his whole life. It is a kind of auditing under the headings of "loss" and "gain" (vv. 7–8). Perhaps the forced inactivity of imprisonment contributed to Paul's taking stock of himself (cf. 2:13–14); a more important factor is his need to foster proper attitudes in the community at Philippi. Thus he prays that they may grow in understanding (1:10) and urges right attitudes among them (2:2–5; 3:15); he makes repeated reference to his personal convictions in today's passage and even points out that the attitude of Christ was the first step in his journey down to death and up to lordship (2:6).

A first major conclusion of Paul's accounting is that his life follows the pattern marked out by this journey of Christ, in 2:6–11. As Christ made no claims based on prior existence (2:6–7), so Paul considers his previous life as loss (3:7). Christ "was found" as a man (2:7); Paul wishes to "be found" in Christ (3:9). Christ took the "form" of a slave (2:7); Paul wishes to be "formed" into the pattern of Christ's death (3:10). Christ received the title "Lord" (2:11); Paul adopts the unusual reference "my Lord" Jesus Christ (3:8). Christ went up to exaltation (2:9); Paul transforms his horizontal imagery of running a race (3:12–14) into an "upward calling" (3:14).

Secondly, Paul emphasizes his difference from Christ in that Paul has not yet reached the goal. Pagan cults of his day stressed the fullness of communion with the divinity which was possessed by the "perfect," those fully initiated into the cult of a god. Paul is willing to refer to some Christians as "perfect" (v. 15; cf. also 1 Cor. 2:6), but their achievement lies in the paradoxical realization that they are not yet perfected (Phil. 3:12, 15). For such as these, to die is "gain" (1:21). But the major redirection of one's life has already been made (3:8); one moves upward (v. 14) because he already experiences the power of Christ's resurrection together with the sharing in his sufferings (v. 10).

A third major consideration draws a further distinction between Christian life and pagan religion. In an epistle where attitudes and understanding assume such importance, the meaning of "knowledge" must be properly qualified. Pagan cults may impart secret "knowledge" to those initiated, but for Paul the knowledge of Jesus Christ "surpasses" (v. 8). This knowledge is further clarified through the concept "faith in Christ" (v. 9); in fact, the two notions are juxtaposed in v. 10. Such an association in effect removes from knowledge any air of the esoteric; it is as accessible as faith itself, which is open to all (Rom. 3:22–24). Further, this qualification of knowledge through the concept of faith allows it to part company with a Jewish understanding of man's relationship with God. This faith is the work of God, grounding a special "righteousness"

(3:9) or relationship with God which is so much the work of God that Paul's fulfillment of the Jewish law was not a part of it. Here the role of man is primarily passive (v. 8, "I have suffered the loss"; v. 9, "so that I might be found in him"; v. 10, "being formed into the pattern"; v. 12, "I have been grasped"), but he is made to undertake the journey of Christ in a manner requiring continued struggle and effort (vv. 12–14).

While stressing the imperfection of man's present condition, Paul also emphasizes how much man has already received through the gift of God's "peace." It is given in answer to every prayer (4:7), in such a way that the Christian can express gratitude as soon as he asks (4:6). As a gift "surpassing" all understanding (4:7), it partakes of the "surpassing" knowledge of Christ (3:8) and presents God's gift of "righteousness" as a developing reality, expressed in a peace which grows with each advance in true knowledge (4:9) and which God can bestow ever more fully on his church (1:2; cf. also 1:6).

Gospel: Luke 20:9–19. Although Matthew and Mark present this parable as directed to members of the supreme council or Sanhedrin (Matt. 21:23; Mark 11:27), Luke explicitly includes the people as members of the audience (20:9). In this gospel, the wicked tenants are the people as a whole; thus Luke avoids expanding the image of the vineyard to signify Israel, unlike Matthew and Mark, for whom the people are the vineyard and the tenants are the leaders (cf. Matt. 21:3; Mark 12:1; Isa. 5:1–2). Luke sustains this focus on the people; they recoil from the lesson of the parable that the gospel must be brought to the Gentiles (v. 16; it is clear from the parallel in Acts 22:21–22 that Luke understands the lesson in this way). Only at the end of this reading does Luke return to the understanding of Matthew and Mark that the leaders were the ones addressed (v. 19). Thus the wicked tenants become an ambivalent image in Luke, pointing both to the people and to their leaders. This appears strange in Luke, since the leaders are several times pictured as fearful of the people, who are in admiration of Jesus (v. 19; cf. also 19:47–48; 22:2, 6). This instability of the people brings us close to the outlook of John (cf. John 2:24–25), but, more important for Luke, prepares for the fulfillment of OT prophecy by involving the people in the guilt for Christ's death (cf. Acts 4:25–27). Further, Luke's emphasis on the people also supports his theme that Jesus' ministry in the temple was fully public (cf. Luke 20:26, 45; 21:38) and that thus there is no basis for regarding the teaching of Jesus as subversive. A still further reason for Luke's emphasis on the people as Jesus' audience during those final days is his desire to show that God had indeed been faithful to his OT promises in making Israel the receiver of his special blessing (cf. Acts 13:46).

The foregoing emphasis on Lucan theology should not obscure the widespread agreement that this is a genuine parable which Jesus spoke and which Matthew, Mark, and Luke modified in various ways. As originally delivered, this parable would have contained little or no allegory. It was based on the situation of an absentee landlord who sent various servants and finally his son to collect the rents; at the sight of the latter, the tenants would have presumed the owner was dead and that the murder of the son would give them first claim to ownerless property. The parable might have originally contained an allusion to Jesus' forthcoming death, but perhaps not. The original ending in v. 15 may have presented the murder of the son as a symbolic expression of consummate wickedness, a total rejection of God's approach to man.

Such a parable as this lent itself easily to further allegorizing; it has happened in all three synoptic gospels, but least of all in Luke. The sending of servants recalls God's intervention in Israel's history (compare the long "period" and harvest "time" in Luke 20:9–10 with the "periods or times" in Acts 1:7), but the comparison is only lightly drawn since the abuse they suffered does not reflect the murder of the prophets or of John the Baptist (cf. Luke 9:9; 11:49–51).

Later allegorizing up till the time of the evangelist readily extended also to the person of Christ, who is understood in the expression "beloved Son" (v. 13; cf. 3:22). Also, the son is killed outside the city (contrast Mark 12:8), with a correspondence to the death of Christ (John 19:17; Heb. 13:12). Christological emphasis was also furthered through the addition of a reference to the keystone, understood as the risen Christ. Unlike Matthew and Mark, Luke omits the note of "marvel" from this citation of Ps. 118 (Luke 20:17) in order to preserve his tone of judgment against the people, and adds instead a more threatening reference, drawn from Isa. 8:14 and Dan. 2:44–45 (Luke 20:18).

HOMILETICAL INTERPRETATION

In the new lectionary design, the Fifth Sunday in Lent is no longer called "Passion Sunday." This designation has been moved ahead to the next Sunday as an optional title for the traditional Palm Sunday. No doubt this shift is designed to bring "Passion Sunday" closer to the tragic events of "Passion Week."

No single theme dominates and unites this set of lessons. The OT reading from Isaiah is the purest form of good news. It declares the gospel of God's deliverance in nonchristological language, but the Christian community cannot fail to read it in the light of that deliverance of Good Friday and Easter soon to be celebrated. The Second Lesson, as with the First Sunday in Lent, contains a clear declaration of the Pauline doctrine of "righteousness by faith" as against "righteousness by law," though there is a secondary theme here which touches upon the nature of the life which flows from faith. The gospel is as pure in its pronouncement of judgment as is the First Lesson in its announcement of deliverance. The parable of the wicked husbandmen lends weight to the traditional Latin name for this Sunday: *Judica*—"Judge me, O God: and plead my cause against an ungodly nation." We are to hear these opening words of the introit as though they came from the lips of Jesus who, like the "beloved Son" in the Gospel parable, is about to be slain by his own people. But *we* are "judged," too, as we contemplate the inhospitality of our own lives to this One whom God has sent.

First Lesson. The verses appointed for this lection represent only a clipping from a group of magnificent prophetic oracles. As a prelude to his work on this text, the preacher should let the whole of chap. 43 speak to him. It is a resounding word of promise to an embattled people. Israel languishes in her Babylonian exile, but this majestic poetry trumpets unconquerable hope. Let her darkness be ever so impenetrable. Let the way home from exile seem ever so impassable. Let her sense of abandonment be ever so total. God flings into the face of all Israel's hopelessness a simple but powerful affirmation: "Fear not, for I am with you" (v. 5). Those whom God has chosen, he will never abandon. In the very act of creating Israel a people, he has pledged himself to her forever.

The temptation to occupy a large block of sermon time describing in great detail Israel's historical situation in the Babylonian period should be resisted. It is much more important to find ways of evoking a sense of the "exile" in which we and our people live today. It is, of course, an exile which is spiritual or relational rather than geographical. Certainly the exiles of our modern world are not only those tragic millions who have been uprooted from their homes and herded behind barbed wire. As we all know, the plushest house in the greenest suburb can be a place of exile. We live in alienation from each other, from ourselves and from God. Often the burden of our past holds us in bondage, or we are trapped in present circumstances outside our control.

But having held up this mirror to human existence, we need to proclaim with equal clarity the powerful "Yes!" by which God negates all the negativities in which our lives are caught: "Fear not, for I am with you." Isaiah pointed Israel back to the previous act of deliverance by which God had created her a people—the exodus. But this was no time for merely remembering. Memory was the basis for hope. God has in store "a new thing" which will dwarf all his previous acts of deliverance (vv. 18, 19). In fact, it should be noted that the tense of the verbs in v. 19 is *present!* The word of this text for every person or community is this: "When you have assessed your situation, explored every possibility, measured every resource and find the prospect hopeless, you have still failed to take into account the one reality which makes a radical difference. God is present and active; and even while you wrestle with futility, he is at work doing a new thing."

The prophet, of course, articulates his message of hope in terms of his own point in history. The Christian preacher looks back in memory not primarily to the exodus but to the "new thing" God accomplished in the death and resurrection of Jesus. We are again about to see how the cry of desolation out of the thick darkness of Golgotha—"My God, my God, why hast thou forsaken me?"—is transformed into the amazing announcement, "He is risen!" as day breaks over the garden. We know Israel's "Redeemer" (v. 14) by a new "name which is above every name." There is One with us who is *the* "way" in the wilderness of this world and who offers himself as "living water" in the midst of our deserts (v. 19). All Isaiah's images offer themselves to the preacher with new depth and power in the light of the mighty act of deliverance the church is preparing to celebrate.

Second Lesson. This extraordinarily rich text (the Ash Wednesday Second Lesson in the traditional lectionary) presents the preacher with an array of thematic stopping points. In the scope of seven verses, Paul introduces such key matters as "the knowledge of Christ," "righteousness," the mystical participation in Christ's sufferings, the resurrection, and the problematic issue of Christian perfection. Any one of these items is more than deserving of a sermon, and the preacher may decide to focus sharply on such a circumscribed theme, keeping in mind the larger context of Paul's whole discussion in this part of Philippians.

It is also possible to take up this passage in its entirety, and here there is a special challenge for the preacher to work through with his people the perennial issue of the relationship between God's grace and man's work. Paul makes it clear that works count for nothing in the matter of justification, or, as it is defined in this text, "righteousness"; yet, it is equally true that the justified man will work more arduously than ever for all that is good. Paul states the paradox with particular sharpness in these verses, and a sermon might be constructed as an exposition of both its sides.

On the one hand, it is clear that *all is of God.* This passage is one of the most powerful statements in the NT of the utter worthlessness of all human achievement as a means of access to God. Paul uses himself as "Exhibit A." Everything which, by human standards, should count with God, he could claim (vv. 4–6). Now Christ has devalued all this, not only back to "ground zero" but to a minus point. They are actually "loss," "refuse" ("rubbish" or "dung" would be more literal), because insofar as a person is depending upon any such illusory supports, there is no chance that he will lean his life on Christ. All of us want to bring some such credentials to God—decency, respectability, reputation, a record of achievement or service. But as capital to purchase our standing with God, they are "dung," i.e., an offense to him, because they are a sign that we are unwilling to trust his offer of free grace in Christ. Thus, the gospel has a radical way of turning all our supposed credits into debits —and then declaring that our debt is canceled!

On the other hand, this passage makes it clear that there is a secondary sense in which *all is of man.* The "I's" that crowd this passage should be noted. Likewise, attention should be given to the muscular nature of the verbs: "that I may gain," "that . . . I may attain," "I press on," "straining forward." The dominant metaphor is that of an Olympic runner, with months of arduous training behind him, stretching every muscle, draining every ounce of energy and every breath of air, in his drive to break the tape. Paul's own rigorously disciplined and vigorously active life provides concrete substance for this image, as do the lives of many saints ancient and modern. The grace which saves doesn't tranquillize; it galvanizes. This free gift is at the same moment the most compelling catalyst of discipline and service—not *so that* "righteousness" will be achieved but *because* it has already been granted. Yet, there is never any doubt where the ultimate priority lies; always at the source of all Christian prayer and action in the gracious God who, by the initiating power of his Spirit, stirs and supports our spirits. Nowhere is this paradox which underlies the whole range of the life of the church and its members put more succinctly than in an earlier sentence of this same letter: "Work out your own salvation with fear and trembling; for God is at work in you both to will and to work for his good pleasure" (2:12, 13).

Gospel. Whatever questions of form (see exegesis) are to be raised about this "parable," there is no question that Luke hears Jesus using it to throw down a radical challenge to the people and leaders of Israel. They are the appointed custodians of "the vineyard of the Lord," but the record of their stewardship is stained with blood. The culmination of their perfidy will be their brutal murder of the owner's son, a turn in the story in which the early church was quick to see "christological" meaning. Inexorable judgment awaits this final act of rebellion. The owner's incredible patience ends, and the "stone" which has been thrown out of the vineyard is hurled back with crushing force. Luke's concluding sentence (v. 19) indicates that the story precipitated the very behavior it was designed to challenge.

Today the target to which we direct our preaching on this parable has shifted. Its word of judgment is not aimed at some outside group, hostile to the claims of the gospel. To direct this message against the secularists, the Communists, or any other "opponents" of Jesus and his kingdom is to deflect it from its true mark. To borrow a phrase, "the enemy is within." That is to say, those who bear responsibility for the life of the church, God's "new Israel," must hear the warning which resounds from this parable. It calls into radical question *our* stewardship in "the vineyard of the Lord." Do we stifle renewal and mission with our conventionality and resistance to change? Do we reject *him*, the Son, in our rejection of the "renegade" people of our society—the unwashed and unwanted? Are we stumbling on the foundation stone, the "rock of our salvation," when we place such heavy value on success, prestige, respectability that we run away from risk, defeat, the cross?

Probably no better commentary on this parable exists than Dostoevsky's chapter "The Grand Inquisitor" in *The Brothers Karamazov*. Jesus returns unexpectedly to medieval Seville. His silent presence throws the establishment into panic. The old bishop has him hauled into the dungeons. There he assails him for having dared to come back to challenge the institution which has been built in his name: "Why, then, art thou come to hinder us?" And he closes the interview with the promise of a second Golgotha: "Tomorrow I shall burn thee. Dixi."[1]

The preacher will find his own way of putting the searching question, Does the Lord of the church fare any better as he comes among his own people today? We live in the church without any guarantee that he may not be preparing new movements in unexpected quarters to replace an "establishment" which has become so entrenched as to reject him. Periodically, the vineyard requires the rooting out of what is old and dead and the pruning of what is still alive so that "out of Jesse" a new vine may spring up, bearing fruit for its Maker and Master "a hundredfold."

1. Fedor Dostoevsky, *The Brothers Karamazov* (New York: The Modern Library), pp. 297, 309.